"Like few others, Schultze ha[s] from the content of his field the storehouse of his deep Ch[r] has been written about how t engaged listener, this book r ..... to communicate in transparent an[d] ...[li]fe-giving ways—particularly in a world that seems to be increasingly divided and often despairing."
—**Karen A. Longman**, Azusa Pacific University

"Schultze has done it again! I believe that this special book will lead all who read it to treasure and use well this gift of communication that God has given us."
—**Kathleen Sindorf**, Cornerstone University

"This book is perfect for college students, church leaders, and practitioners seeking a theologically sound approach to improving communication through a growing heart and focused practice. It weaves the inner attitudes Christians need—gratitude, discretion, listening, and humility—with practical application in community, storytelling, and media use."
—**Elizabeth McLaughlin**, Bethel University

"This wonderful book draws from our Christian tradition of both listening and expressing ourselves, giving it current application through various means—from silence to smartphones. It makes us better communicators and even guides us to become better people."
—**Terry Lindvall**, Virginia Wesleyan College

"All of us need this book, but particularly young readers experiencing fear, anxiety, and depression in a society where people increasing 'shoot' (with words and other things) before thinking. Schultze calls us to communicate from our brokenness, our deepest souls. It's the kind of communication for which God made us—and which we crave."
—**Michael Longinow**, Biola University

"Students have grown confident and mindful under Schultze's guidance—more prone to embrace virtue and less to admire just technique. This book is a fresh look at the human condition through the eyes of a soulful scholar who writes well for all audiences."
—**Mark Fackler**, Calvin University (emeritus)

"Schultze has influenced my understanding of communication and of teaching more than anyone. If I had only one communication text to teach any class in the discipline, this would be my choice."
—**Dan Fultz**, Cedarville University

"Drawing from a lifetime of teaching and scholarship, Schultze models the intelligence, wisdom, and Christlike vulnerability that we need today more than ever."

—**Naaman Wood**, Redeemer University, Ontario

"Weaving together poignant personal stories and a careful reading of Scripture, Schultze offers a rich tapestry of insights that invite us all to communicate with grace and virtue."

—**David Balzer**, Canadian Mennonite University

"This is a comprehensive, compelling introduction to the gift, ministry, and joys of communication. It is a veritable treasure chest of definitions worth remembering, stories worth retelling, and challenges worth pondering."

—**Paul Patton**, Spring Arbor University

"What a gracious call to consider the God-given roots of communication and our ongoing responsibility to measure our rhetoric. Highly recommended."

—**Craig Detweiler**, author of *iGods: How Technology Shapes Our Spiritual and Social Lives*

"This book is immensely helpful and illuminating to anyone aspiring to be an effective communicator. Schultze's skills as a scholar and as a professional communicator shine on every page."

—**Benson Fraser**, Virginia Wesleyan University

"Our culture uses words to divide and conquer. We prize rhetoric that is accented with sarcasm and loaded with cynicism. It happens in our families, our jobs, our politics, and our churches. Schultze makes a compelling case for another way: servant communication. Brilliant in its simplicity, Schultze's book is utterly transformational."

—**David McFadzean**, writer and film and TV producer (*Home Improvement*)

"This book is a thought-provoking reflection on how Christ-centered convictions can season all of our interactions. It is for everyone wondering what it looks and sounds like to communicate in a way that conveys the wisdom and joy of the Lord."

—**Josh Danaher**, Grand Canyon University

"Schultze braids together relatable personal and contemporary examples, ancient biblical and theological wisdom, and relevant communication scholarship and theory. This three-strand cord makes this text a must-read for Christians vested in the practice and study of good communication."

—**Jonathan Pettigrew**, Arizona State University

COMMUNICATING
with GRACE *and*
VIRTUE

COMMUNICATING *with* GRACE *and* VIRTUE

Learning to LISTEN, SPEAK, TEXT, and INTERACT *as a Christian*

Quentin J. Schultze

B
Baker Academic
a division of Baker Publishing Group
Grand Rapids, Michigan

Published by Baker Academic
a division of Baker Publishing Group
PO Box 6287, Grand Rapids, MI 49516-6287
www.bakeracademic.com

Printed in the United States of America

Library of Congress Cataloging-in-Publication Data
Names: Schultze, Quentin J. (Quentin James), 1952– author.
Title: Communicating with grace and virtue : learning to listen, speak, text, and
    interact as a Christian / Quentin J. Schultze.
Description: Grand Rapids, Michigan : Baker Academic, a division of Baker
    Publishing Group, 2020.
Identifiers: LCCN 2020011344 | ISBN 9781540961273 (paperback) | ISBN
    9781540963413 (hardcover)
Subjects: LCSH: Communication—Religious aspects—Christianity.
Classification: LCC BV4597.53.C64 S378 2020 | DDC 248.4—dc23
LC record available at https://lccn.loc.gov/2020011344

In keeping with biblical principles of creation stewardship, Baker Publishing Group advocates the responsible use of our natural resources. As a member of the Green Press Initiative, our company uses recycled paper when possible. The text paper of this book is composed in part of post-consumer waste.

20 21 22 23 24 25 26   7 6 5 4 3 2 1

To Elliot James Kim—
"Wow, I wasn't expecting that!"

Contents

Contents

3. Be Responsible   53

4. Address Brokenness   69

Acknowledgments

I would like to thank some of those from among the living "cloud of witnesses" (Heb. 12:1) who have served me generously in the preparation of this book: Josh Danaher, Amy King, Chris Leland, Mike Longinow, Lisa Dunne, Stephanie Bennett, Mary Darling, Diane Badzinski, Gerald Mast, Tom Carmody, Ben Fraser, Dave Hartwell, Sheila Guzman, and Kevin Schut.

Introduction

I once spoke at a Christian university chapel service about how difficult it was for me as a child to communicate with an alcoholic father and a schizophrenic mother. It was the first time I publicly discussed my painful childhood.

Students lined up to speak with me privately after my address. Some tried to hide their tears. Each one told me that family issues made it difficult for them to form deep relationships at college. Even juniors and seniors said that they felt lonely. Some students revealed their depression and anxiety. By speaking transparently about my struggles, I gave them courage to open their hearts about their own.

I knew that I wanted to write this book to help Christians discover the joy of communicating well in spite of fear, loneliness, and brokenness. We all experience challenges that we tend to hide from others instead of seeking healing. I asked God for the courage to write this book, but it still took me decades to be comfortable enough with my own brokenness that I could step out in faith.

In this book I offer many practical tips and engaging examples, often from my own life. Studying communication at a university made me more self-confident. When friends shared the gospel with me, I began integrating my study of communication with my faith in Jesus Christ. I discovered that Scripture offers life-changing communication advice. Step by step, with help and encouragement from others, I learned how to communicate well, both personally and professionally. You can too.

I earned graduate degrees, became a professor of communication, and taught at various Christian universities and seminaries. I also worked as an advertising copywriter, TV and film critic, internet communications consultant, author, and mentor. Grateful to God for each opportunity, I felt called to help others communicate well.

Growing up in a troubled home, I learned not to take communication for granted. Relationships, I found, disintegrate when communication breaks down. Office tensions make work stressful. Arguments weaken marriages. Conflicts split congregations. In the words of Christian physician-psychologist Paul Tournier, "Life is inseparable from conflict."[1]

Why are we not able to communicate better? Are we lazy? Confused? Unskilled? Are our motives warped? All of the above—and more. But our personal brokenness as communicators is not the end of our story.

God offers us the gift of communication so we can serve him and one another. I call it *servant communication*. This book explains servant communication as a way of using God's gift of communication to love God and our neighbors as ourselves (Mark 12:30–31). When we put servant communication into action, we serve others as we would like to be served. We build healthy relationships. We thrive in homes, businesses, classrooms, and churches. We can even climb out of our difficult pasts and discover the joy of open, honest relationships.

Like Old Testament writers, I use the word "shalom" to describe such healthy relationships. I increasingly discovered shalom in my own life as I learned to communicate well. Both professionally and personally, I became a servant communicator, orienting my heart and mind to the love of God, neighbor, and self. Each chapter in this book addresses an aspect of servant communication.

Chapter 1 invites you to accept the call to servant communication, one of the most important skills one can learn in life. Communication is a calling that we all inherit as followers of Jesus Christ. I explore the wide range of communication-related careers and academic majors to show how essential communication really is. God creates for us what communication professor Ryan Montague calls "divine opportunities," even in our everyday conversations.[2]

Chapter 2 addresses the heart of servant communication: gratitude. Scripture says that our words flow from our hearts (Luke 6:45). The more grateful we are, the more we will communicate as neighbor-loving persons rather than self-serving persons. Gratefulness nurtures our desire to use the gift of communication to serve God and neighbors—and to avoid relationships, jobs, and sometimes even churches that make us cynical and critical.

Chapter 3 addresses our responsibility to God. We are created to communicate responsibly in God's name. We are God's caretakers of language, which we can use to care for others with excellence and compassion. "Christian communication" is excellent and compassionate communication.

Chapter 4 examines our brokenness as communicators. We are not merely imperfect communicators; we are sinful ones. We avoid others, lie, and blame. We sin individually and collectively, in small groups and in large organizations. Along the way, we hide our real feelings from others. My parents and I lived in a sin-wrecked family. I had no idea how to serve them—what to say or how to say it. I stopped listening and just criticized them for years.

Chapter 5 relates communication to community, especially shalom. Created in the image and likeness of our triune God, we are designed to live in healthy, life-giving relationships. How we communicate with one another is vitally important for the quality of our shared lives. Servant communication equips us to flourish in communities of shalom.

Chapter 6 considers the importance of personal character in our communication. We communicate as distinct persons, not just for specific goals. Our character speaks. The more Christlike we become, the more we contribute to shalom. I examine some of the fruit of the Spirit as God-given, communication-related virtues. Our character might be our primary witness to the world. Jesus says that we should be known by our love, the essence of Christlikeness (John 13:35).[3]

Chapter 7 examines storytelling, probably the most powerful form of communication. Many of Jesus's teachings were stories (parables). The Bible is the story of God and his people, from the beginning of time forward. Popular culture—represented in media such as movies and TV series—sometimes competes with the gospel, like dueling storytellers. Those who control popular stories in a culture generally have the greatest influence on our values, beliefs, and behaviors. As servant communicators, we can learn how to tell stories well so we can gain people's attention, engage culture, and share our faith.

Chapter 8 looks at communication technologies. More and more of our everyday communication is mediated through digital devices, especially the smartphone. In one sense, new technologies are part of the opening up of God's original creation, offering us new opportunities to love and serve one another. Yet the same technologies can consume too much of our time and lead us to become compulsive users. Writer Stephen King calls the smartphone a "twenty-first-century slave bracelet."[4] As servant communicators, we can wisely adapt technologies for good purposes, fitting our messages with appropriate media.

The biblical themes in this book have long been addressed by servant communicators. I love this ancient monastic saying: "Speak only if you can improve upon the silence."[5] Author Henri Nouwen says that the desert monks who practiced vows of silence "did not think of solitude as being alone, but as being alone with God."[6] Imagine the potential impact of such age-old wisdom on today's public discourse, especially politics and journalism. We can learn about communication both from Scripture and from other servant communicators throughout history.

Readers will discover my enormous debt to St. Augustine of Hippo. I read two of his books annually: *On Christian Teaching* (or *Doctrine*)[7] and *Confessions*. Augustine was trained as a rhetorician (public persuader) before he became a Christian. At first, he wondered if he could be a Christian and a professional communicator at the same time. Fortunately for us, he not only concluded that he could but he also proceeded to write books and sermons that addressed biblical truths about communication.

19

As I explain in later chapters, one of the great blessings of the gift of language is that we can communicate through history and across generations. With biblical discernment, we can distinguish between what church historian Jaroslav Pelikan calls *tradition* (the living faith of the dead) and *traditionalism* (the dead faith of the living).[8] We Christians negotiate all of our discernment through communication with God, one another, and ourselves. It is a stunning gift that we generally take for granted.

If you wish to contact me, please visit my website at www .quentinschultze.com. There you can also find multimedia materials for use with this book and others I have written, including materials for instructors and group leaders.

I am still surprised that I became a communication scholar and teacher. I believe that God directed me to study communication both to renew my own life and to use me to teach others how to communicate with grace and virtue. Communication is a wonderful gift. I gratefully accept it and seek to use it wisely as a caretaker of God's Word and world. That is why I began speaking openly about my life challenges and why I thank God for every person who courageously shares their heart with me after my speeches. Thank you for joining me on this journey of becoming a servant communicator. I pray that you will be surprised by joy along the way.

1

Accept the Call

Now when the LORD spoke to Moses in Egypt, he said to him, "I am the LORD. Tell Pharaoh king of Egypt everything I tell you." But Moses said to the LORD, "Since I speak with faltering lips, why would Pharaoh listen to me?"

—Exodus 6:28–30

My life has been both challenging and rewarding. My father was an alcoholic and my mother was a paranoid schizophrenic. In high school, I never attended a social event. I was too socially awkward and introverted. I had only one date; her parents told me never to ask her out again.

While I was studying communication at a university, some friends shared the gospel with me. I learned, as Henri Nouwen puts it, that "conversion is the individual equivalent of revolution."[1] My new faith in Jesus Christ gave me hope. Studying Scripture and communication at the same time became a wonderful blessing—a double revolution in my life. I was like an explorer in a new land of grace, reporting to friends what I was discovering about God, communication, and myself.

God called me, a reluctant communicator, to teach others to communicate. I felt like Moses: "God, send someone else!" I eventually became a professor of communication. Along the way, I learned how to practice what I was teaching.

I discovered that communication is essential in nearly all careers and certainly in every personal and professional relationship. I believe that God calls us to become effective communicators so we can serve him and one another in all areas of life.

In this opening chapter, I invite you personally to accept the call to communicate well, as a faithful follower of Jesus Christ. We do not have to be perfect communicators. We seek steady progress, not perfection; we are pilgrim communicators assisted by the Holy Spirit. Communication is too important to take for granted. It is a gift from God that we can develop, enjoy, and use to serve others as we would like to be served. I call it servant communication.

Communicating for Life

Communication is not just a skill for a few people and a handful of careers. Nearly everything we do is communicative in nature, including making friends, interviewing for jobs, watching videos, and falling in love. Most importantly, communication equips us to grow relationally with God. We are designed to communicate like fish are created to swim. As I explain later, human communication is how we create shared understanding (or shared meaning) to accomplish many things.

The Bible tells the story of communication between God and humankind. It describes both faithful people who listen to God and unfaithful people who ignore or defy God. It portrays both wise communicators who listen before speaking and foolish ones who speak before listening. Scripture shows us that we are made in the image and likeness of a God who spoke the world into existence, became the Word made flesh, and shared his word with us through Scripture.[2]

When our communication sours, our lives become miserable; we face conflicts, loneliness, and sometimes despair. But when our communication is healthy, we enjoy friends, family, and coworkers. We also have greater self-confidence to live faithfully. We naturally enjoy communicating with God, others, and even ourselves. We experience real life.

To use a sports metaphor, communication is central to the game of life. Charging ahead in life without developing our communication abilities is like running onto a sports field without knowing how to play the game.

Communication is an essential skill for nearly every career. Organizations of all kinds seek employees who can listen carefully, speak well, write clearly, and interact cross-culturally. Employers seek people who can communicate with coworkers, customers, and clients. Media networks often employ skilled storytellers, not just technical producers.

The apostle Paul's letters to churches highlight healthy communication. Early believers needed to learn how to encourage one another and solve disputes. They had to listen, teach, and testify in different settings. They had to learn what

We All Are Rhetoricians

Today, people use the word "rhetoric" negatively to refer to manipulative and self-serving communication. But the study of oral (vs. written) rhetoric began before the birth of Jesus Christ among ancient Greek and Roman *orators* (skilled public speakers, also called rhetors), who developed the art of *rhetoric* (public persuasion). Aristotle (384–322 BC), sometimes called the father of Western philosophy, classically defined rhetoric as "the possible means of persuasion in a given situation."[a]

Roman orator Cicero (106–43 BC) said that there are three major purposes for rhetoric—to inform, to persuade, and to delight. Most human communication, including media, falls into one or more of those rhetorical categories. Long before Jesus was born, then, rhetoric had become a scholarly field. Rhetoric, as communication, is one of the oldest academic disciplines.

By the twentieth century, scholars from many different academic disciplines had studied language and other forms of human communication, creating a field called communication studies. It includes both social-scientific research in psychology and sociology and insights from the humanities, including philosophy, literature, linguistics, and the arts. One of the most important contributions from the ancient rhetoricians was the recognition that communication is crucial for representative democracy, where leaders publicly debate and where courts consider justice.

The apostle Paul relied significantly on ancient rhetorical techniques to communicate truth.[b] After studying their culture and communication, Paul addressed philosophers on Mars Hill (Acts 17:16–34). Saint Augustine (AD 354–430), who wrote the first major book on the art of rhetoric for Christians, said that Christians should be the most effective rhetoricians because they know the truth and are called by God to share it.[c]

Moreover, the Greek word for "persuasion" (*peitho*) comes from the same root as the Latin word for "faith." Aristotle's term for rhetorical "proof" is the related word *pistis*, which eventually meant the highest form of Christian knowledge.[d]

a. Aristotle, *The Art of Rhetoric*, ed. Harvey Yunis, trans. Robin Waterfield (Oxford: Oxford University Press, 2018), 6.

b. Jeffrey A. D. Weima, "What Does Aristotle Have to Do with Paul? An Evaluation of Rhetorical Criticism," *Calvin Theological Journal* 32, no. 2 (1997): 458–68.

c. Augustine, *On Christian Teaching* 4.2.3, trans. R. P. H. Green (New York: Oxford University Press, 1997), 101.

d. Kenneth Burke, *A Rhetoric of Motives* (Berkeley: University of California Press, 1969), 52.

Paul calls "being all things to all people" (1 Cor. 9:22).[3] He was the first great communication strategist in the church, adapting the gospel message to various audiences ("all people").

Today, much of our communication requires us to understand and serve people from different cultures. Because of worldwide transportation and communication technologies, learning how to adapt our messages to different audiences is critically important.

Celebrated media theorist Marshall McLuhan called the international communication system a "global village."[4] It is a catchy metaphor. But it makes more sense to describe our technologically interconnected world as something like a "global city," filled with "neighborhoods" that speak different languages, believe different things, and often defend their cultures against outside media influence.

In addition, the globalization of media does not necessarily make it easier for us to understand those whom we hear about through news and see in entertainment. Greater messaging does not automatically produce deeper understanding. Communication scholar James W. Carey says that "modern technology actually makes communication much

Careers and Subfields in Communication Studies—Part 1

- *Interpersonal communication*—person to person
- *Small-group communication*—about three to eight persons
- *Listening*—understanding others, not just hearing them
- *Storytelling*—through media as well as in person
- *Health communication*—using all forms and media of communication to promote personal and community health
- *Sports communication*—including on-air talent, sports reporting, and professional and collegiate public relations
- *Leadership communication*—helping individuals and organizations use communication to define, share, and achieve their goals
- *Organizational communication*—serving organizations with internal communication (e.g., to employees) and external communication (e.g., to various "publics," such as stockholders and news media)

Note: The breadth of communication disciplines and communication-related careers is amazing. The three lists in this chapter only touch the surface.

more difficult. Rational agreement and democratic coherence become problematic when so little background is shared in common."[5]

Moreover, we dwell largely in "secular" societies, and we learn to think and speak as secular people regardless of our faith. Missionary-theologian Lesslie Newbigin observes that those who are raised in the church actually grow up "bilingual." He says we Christians "use the mother tongue of the Church on Sundays, but for the rest of our lives we use the language imposed by the occupying power" (the wider culture).[6]

The field of communication studies is so vast that we can simply add the word "communication" to practically any

The Religious Origins of Communication Theories

James W. Carey says that there are two basic theories (or views) of communication—cultural and transmission. A *cultural view,* which he ties historically to the Roman Catholic faith, emphasizes ritual; it looks at communication as participation in a meaningful ritual, whether having an everyday conversation or reading a news report. In other words, to understand communication we have to look at how we do it routinely, like a ritual. A *transmission view,* which he connects to Protestantism, emphasizes sending messages to influence others. Carey cites evangelism as an example. Both views can help us understand specific forms of communication, regardless of their apparent religious origins.[a]

a. James W. Carey, *Communication as Culture: Essays on Media and Society* (Boston: Unwin Hyman, 1989), 18.

human endeavor. More than likely, scholars have already been studying it. We can investigate mealtime communication, neighborhood communication, parenting communication, dating communication, friendship communication, coaching communication, and worship communication. In other words, learning how to communicate well applies to almost everything we do professionally and personally.

Communicating in Culture

How could one human ability—communication—become so essential to practically all we do? The simple answer is that God created us to relate to him and one another. We are social creatures designed to enjoy, love, and serve one another. We interact through communication.

Careers and Subfields in Communication Studies— Part 2

- *Family communication*—relational dynamics that enhance or diminish family life
- *Journalism*—print, broadcast, and digital media reporting and commentary
- *Public relations*—developing and maintaining favorable public images for persons and organizations as well as responding to crises
- *Advertising*—promoting products, services, and ideas to selected audiences through various media
- *Cross-cultural communication*—how to understand, address, overcome, and affirm cultural differences among communicators
- *Social media*—using many forms of aural, visual, and textual messages in digital media

A more complicated answer is that we are cultural creatures. We are not as driven by DNA as other creatures. Our creaturely instincts do not dictate how we communicate. Instead, we use communication to create dynamic *cultures*— entire ways of life.[7] We also use communication to modify our cultures and to pass them along from generation to generation and place to place. A culture includes a people's values, practices, and beliefs, along with all physical things like dwellings, clothing, and technologies. As a whole, human culture includes everything on earth that would not be here apart from human activity: from selfies and video streaming to worship music and fast food. Without communication, we could not create and share culture. With communication, we together can change what we believe and do in life. We all are called to create culture and to participate in sharing culture, such as by sharing our beliefs and values with our children.

As we communicate, we create, maintain, and change our ways of life. We work, play, and simply live together. In other words, our communication is always cultural.[8] This is why learning another language includes learning another culture.

When God created the world, he called human beings to take care of it. The book of Genesis uses the language of agriculture—cultivating in the Garden of Eden (Gen. 2:15). We humans care for all kinds of culture, from movies to games and sports. As I write this, and as you read it, we together are cultivating a biblical understanding of communication. In our congregations, we cultivate a shared understanding of who we are as God's people, using psalms, hymns, and other songs, as well as sermons and Bible studies.

In short, we are called to use communication to cultivate God-glorifying ways of life—and to thank God along the way both for the opportunity and for all positive results. Much of our everyday communication is *pre-evangelistic*— creating the kinds of Christlike relationships and cultures that attract nonbelievers. All of our communication can contribute to or detract from God's kingdom on earth. Communication equips us to be agents of renewal in a broken world. Writer Andy Crouch says that we should "wake up every morning eager to create [culture]."[9]

Learning Great Communication

As with all cultural activities, communication is learned. Although learning a first language comes naturally, excellent human communication requires dedication and effort. As Scripture shows, people have trouble listening to God and one another. Misunderstanding and deception are common.

Even Jesus's disciples often misunderstood him (see, e.g., Luke 9:45; 24:25), and he certainly had communication skills beyond ours!

Each of us has communication strengths, and we can strive to improve in the communication categories where we are weak. For example, we can learn how to interpret and evaluate media stories. What are plays, movies, and television shows telling us about gender, romance, happiness, and vengeance? How do they support or challenge a biblical worldview? Such media discernment (often called media criticism) is crucial for a life of faith. Otherwise we implicitly learn to be like the broader culture rather than like faithful, holy Christians. Instead of just living *in* the world, we end up being merely *of* the world (John 17:11–18).

Similarly, we can practice listening, analyzing, discussing, and persuading. We can learn how to seek and offer forgiveness. We can learn how to share our faith, part of which

Strategic Communication

Becoming a good communicator requires more than specialized skills. We can learn an overall planning process often called *strategic communication*. The basics are similar to ancient rhetoric:

- Know your audience.
- Know your communication purpose.
- Know your message.
- Adapt your message to your audience.
- Determine the best media to use for the message and audience.
- Get audience feedback to evaluate your efforts.
- Use your findings to adjust your messaging for greater effectiveness.

includes knowing when it is appropriate to do so. We can learn how to use communication to grow our relationships with God, friends, family, faith communities, and coworkers.

We cannot become experts in all forms of communication, but we can become competent in many of them, especially as our careers change. Studies show that under half—and perhaps as few as 27 percent—of university students end up in careers directly related to their academic majors.[10] Even so, nearly everyone ends up in a communication-related career because communication is so important in nearly all work.

Communicating Courageously

Superficial, routine communication is not so difficult. We all do it adequately most of the time. Someone asks us, "Would you please pass the salt?" We understand, and we pass the salt. That kind of simple transaction requires more courtesy than skill.

But a lot of communication requires courage, especially if we lack experience. Job interviews create anxiety for most of us. What about asking others out on a date, especially if we do not know them well? It took more courage than I had in the beginning of my adult life. I feared rejection.

After writing a book on TV evangelists, I started receiving requests for media interviews. I was doing so many of them that I was no longer paying close attention to who was interviewing me and who the audience was. I discovered halfway through one radio show that I was being interviewed by someone in the nation of New Zealand, not in the Michigan town of Zeeland only twenty miles from me. I still feel like a fool when I recall the episode decades later. My answers were so tuned to an American audience that the program host finally asked me, "Dr. Schultze, do you know where New Zealand is?" I later discovered that the popular morning show was broadcast to millions across New Zealand. I feared doing more media interviews.

In college I gave a terrible presentation as part of a group project. I let my whole team down. For a while after that experience, I feared participating in any group presentations.

We can move ahead courageously even when our fears are deep. I had to work at getting over my fear of teaching by doing it one class session at a time. If we are fearful group leaders, we can still learn how to become better ones. That recognition alone can embolden us.

I am not naturally a good listener, partly because I fear that new information will challenge my existing assumptions. What if I learn something that shows I have been teaching and writing erroneously for years? It happens. I need courage to listen outside of my comfort zone.

Most of the communication situations that we think are crucially important and make us fearful are not so significant in the long run. Our future does not depend only on our personal communication, such as giving a great or mediocre speech. We can also find courage in the fact that most people want us to succeed and are generously forgiving and encouraging.

Examining Our Motives

The most life-changing truth about communication is deeply biblical. As Jesus puts it, our words flow from the desires of

Careers and Subfields in Communication Studies—Part 3

- *Homiletics*—ways and means of effective preaching
- *Educational communication*—fostering classroom and online instruction
- *Film and video*—creating long and short moving-image messages, especially for mass and social media
- *Media criticism*—interpreting, understanding, and evaluating media messages
- *Public speaking*—presenting in front of large and small audiences
- *Rhetorical theory and criticism*—using ancient and modern techniques for assessing how, how well, and how ethically people use messages to influence others
- *Graphic arts and multimedia*—designing visual messages, from organizational logos to brochures, posters, websites, TV graphics, and video games
- *Business communication*—from writing to marketing, brand management, event planning, and customer relations

our hearts (Matt. 12:34). Our motives, not just our messages, are critically important.

The sad truth is that we all have some selfish and even evil desires. We do not always use the gift of communication to love God and our neighbors as ourselves. We miss our true calling. As Augustine put it, we fail to offer love and compassion to those to whom it is due—namely, *everyone*, even our enemies.[11]

We live in a time of deeply fractured communication. Many of us do not trust public communicators. Politics is filled with half-truths and personal attacks. Hollywood often

What Motivates Us?

One of the greatest rhetorical theorists of the twentieth century, Kenneth Burke, developed a "dramatist" theory of human communication that captures the importance of motive. He describes humans as actors on a stage. We Christians might say that we act on God's stage. "Motive" describes why we do what we do—including why we communicate. What are we trying to accomplish when we communicate? What kind of outcome would we like? Sometimes our motives are obvious, such as trying to present ourselves positively in a job interview to get a position. Other times our motives are complicated, confusing, and even questionably good, such as why we are gossiping with friends. For Burke, human motive is entangled in "guilt" and "redemption."[a]

a. See Kenneth Burke, *A Rhetoric of Motives* (Berkeley: University of California Press, 1969), 31.

exploits rather than serves audiences. Some organizations do not acknowledge receipt of job applications, and a few do not even respond to candidates after giving them interviews.

It is one thing for us to be skilled communicators. It is far more for us to be respectful ones who treat others the way we would like to be treated. Jesus calls us to model skilled communication anchored in right motives.

We are God's ears, eyes, and voices on earth. We are created to be caretakers of God's Word and our own words, verbal and nonverbal, in person and through media. If we do so faithfully, loving God and our neighbors as ourselves, we become salt and light in a world broken by sin. Sometimes we will fail at even basic communication. But if we focus as much on our motives as our skills, we can still rest at night knowing we tried to love God and our neighbors as ourselves.

Conclusion

I had no idea what I was getting into when I realized that I was being called to study and practice communication. I was ill prepared. I felt like Moses; I wanted God to send somebody else. After all, I was starting from a disadvantaged background. I feared even trying to become a professional communicator. I felt guilty about not trusting God to keep my motives pure and to be with me when I would fall.

I identified with Abraham, who the writer of Hebrews says was faithful even though he did not know where he was going (Heb. 11:8). I too was lost, unsure where I was going. But I did desire to glorify God by communicating faithfully in Jesus's name. So I accepted the call to communication. It has been a joy as well as a challenge. As the psalmist puts it, God establishes the work of our hands (Ps. 90:17)—and presumably our mouths and ears as well. I hope you will join me on the journey, accepting the call to become a servant communicator. You will bless others and be blessed in all areas of your life.

FOR DISCUSSION

1. How would you define "servant communication"?

2. What does it mean to be called to communicate?

3. Why do many people use the word "rhetoric" negatively?

4. The apostle Paul says we should be "all things to all people" (1 Cor. 9:22). Should we really be "all things" to all audiences?

5. Do you agree with missionary-theologian Lesslie Newbigin that Christians grow up "bilingual"?

2

Offer Thanks

The good person out of the good treasure of the
heart produces good, and the evil person out of
evil treasure produces evil; for it is out of the
abundance of the heart that the mouth speaks.

—Luke 6:45 NRSV

When I was a university student, I met two young
women from out of town who were visiting my
church. One of them interested me, so I briefly
talked with her. She said she was interviewing locally for a
job and might return.

Several weeks later she started attending my church. I
decided to ask her out for lunch, but as I was feeling socially
awkward I needed considerable courage. My opportunity
finally came at a church social event. My mind was racing

as I tried to think of what to say. I walked up to her, reminded her that we had met, and said, "I recall your yellow dress and lovely legs." She smiled and replied, "That was my friend."

We went to lunch and began dating in spite of that rocky beginning. We have now been married for over forty years. I am thankful that she overlooked my poor communication skills and got to know my heart. She has always been a terrific listener, eventually becoming a hospice chaplain.

This chapter addresses the importance of gratitude in our communication. Our best communication flows from grateful hearts. The more we open our hearts to receive God's blessings, the more fully we can become servant communicators.

Engaging Our Hearts

Jesus says that our words flow from the desires of our hearts (Luke 6:45). I had a heartfelt desire to get to know the woman who eventually became my wife. I was awkward but sincere, with good intentions. I was grateful for her patience and for the grace she extended to me.

Depending on the condition of our hearts, our communication can be good or bad. We can be patient and understanding or hasty and dismissive. Sometimes we pretend to have positive feelings toward others, but eventually our actions reveal our real attitudes toward them. Augustine says, "Human actions can be distinguished only by the love in which they are rooted."[1] When we communicate from our hearts, our minds follow.

We all communicate along a gratitude-ingratitude continuum. On one end is gratitude, which opens our hearts to others. We talk about the good things that are happening in our lives. Sometimes we are even astonished—as I was when my acquaintance agreed to go out to lunch with me. When we are grateful, we tend to hear and see others through a healthy, hopeful lens. Aware of God's goodness in our lives, we treat others as we would like to be treated.

On the other end of the spectrum is ingratitude. It makes us cynical, dismissive, and even critical communicators. We can become bitter when we are unhappy or when we feel unfairly treated. Spending a lot of time with negative people can influence us to become communicators who discourage rather than encourage others. We might become habitually negative persons. Our hearts get warped, and we live in emotional turmoil that infects our communication.

Of course, our life experiences can shape our attitudes. Growing up amid deep family conflicts, I tended to be a highly critical person. I saw people as threats and tried to protect myself by fighting verbally or just ignoring others (fight or flight). My hurting heart made it difficult for me to be transparent and to avoid becoming defensive in response to even minor criticisms.

The Employee Who Was Addicted to Negativity

During high school, I worked in a family-owned pharmacy with wonderful employees—with one exception. This particular employee complained about the owner, customers, and coworkers. He was also a gossip machine, programmed to pass along information that made others look bad and made him look great. The manager talked with him repeatedly about his poor attitude, but it made no difference. Eventually the owner fired him. He seemed to be addicted to negativity.

Receiving Gratitude

We have many reasons to be grateful. Instead of allowing ourselves to become critical persons, we should think about whatever is true, noble, right, pure, lovely, admirable, excellent, and praiseworthy (Phil. 4:8). By dwelling more on life's goodness, we fill our hearts with gratitude and nurture servant communication. Rabbi Abraham Heschel says, "There is a built-in *sense of indebtedness in the consciousness of man,* an awareness of *owing gratitude*, of being *called upon* at certain moments to reciprocate, to answer, to live in a way which is compatible with the grandeur and mystery of living." He says that the "truth of being human is gratitude; its secret is appreciation."[2]

One reason to be grateful is the gift of our communication capacity. Even though we have to learn how to communicate, the capacity is an astonishing gift from God. We do not create that capacity; we accept and develop it.

A second reason for being grateful communicators is that we can communicate about our communication—*metacommunication*. Other creatures cannot. As Kenneth Burke puts it, dogs do not bark about barking.[3] God enables us to understand and improve our communication. We are not limited to stimulus-effect signaling; we are not governed by animalistic habits. We can learn and grow as thankful communicators, talking about and improving our communication. This book is a journey into biblical metacommunication.

A third reason for filling our hearts with gratitude is because we have the Holy Spirit. The Holy Spirit is our advocate, sent from the Father in Jesus's name (John 14:16). The Spirit helps us in our weakness and intercedes for us according to God's will (Rom. 8:26–27).

I believe that when I asked my wife-to-be out for lunch, the Spirit was with us. I cannot otherwise explain what happened. The Spirit must have opened her heart. In purely human terms, my whole approach was misguided. And her charitable response was inexplicable. I should have approached her much more appropriately, but I thank the Spirit for intervening, and I thank her for giving me a chance.

Using Symbols

God's gift of our symbol-using capacity is amazing. All of our communication requires *symbols*—representations of meaning. Every word is a symbol. So are all images used to convey meaning, such as traffic lights, company logos, and T-shirt graphics. Sentences and movies are like strings of interrelated verbal and visual symbols.

God gave various persons names to signify their roles in biblical history. Abram became Abraham when God called him to be the father of many nations (Gen. 17:5). Like our God, we use symbols to identify who and whose we are. At Antioch, the followers of Jesus were first called Christians (Acts 11:26). All of this naming reflects the gift of using symbols.

We are the only species that uses symbols so extensively. We continually create new words and images. By the time a new dictionary comes out, it is already incomplete. No print or online dictionary can capture all the meanings and uses of words—over one million words in English alone.[4] A theory of communication that applies to other creatures is insufficient for understanding those of us made in the image and likeness of God.[5] In fact, there are dozens of theories for human communication, because our God-given gift is so radically different from other creatures' communication.[6] Our metacommunication is strikingly creative.

In Genesis, God brings the animals to Adam to see what he would call them (Gen. 2:19–20). Adam had the freedom to identify each of the species separately with symbols. Genesis suggests that God has given us the gift of symbolic communication so that we might work with and enjoy one another. Once God created Eve, she and Adam could share meaning and understanding like no other species. They could fellowship with each other and with God. They could become true friends.

Employing Verbal and Nonverbal Language

The gift of communication includes the gift of *language*—the many ways we use symbols to communicate. The word "language" has its origin in the Latin word for tongue (*lingua*). Our primary mode of language is speech, but we also use nonverbal communication, from emojis to attire. The ways movies are scripted, edited, and scored are part of the language of moviemaking. The many ways we communicate are all essentially languages—sometimes called "codes."

When I complimented my acquaintance on her legs, I lacked an understanding of dating language—what to say and when and how to say it. I was so inexperienced that I could have failed even more miserably. I was creative but verbally clumsy and potentially offensive. But she read sincerity on my face and was not offended.

We are by nature linguistically creative creatures. We produce podcasts and compose lyrics. We create graphic novels

Why Many Church Doors Are Red

Tom Carmody, Professor of Communication

One of the earliest lessons my wife and I taught our children was to say "please" and "thank you." We wanted to pass down to them what our parents taught us, fostering attitudes of petition and thankfulness.

Such attitudes are essential because our faith journey is not just about us, our denomination, or even our local church. Jesus's church did not begin when our own faith community was founded, when our church was planted, or even when we first believed. We stand on the shoulders of faithful souls who have gone before us.

This is why some church doors are red. They are a reminder for all who gather that they are entering a building to worship, and that the entry fee for that privilege has been purchased by people they may never meet. The red doors are a visual metaphor to remind those who pass through that they enter by the blood of the martyrs. Someone somewhere has paid or is paying the ultimate price for our opportunity to worship. So we keep saying please and thank you.

and YouTube videos. We text messages and deliver group presentations. We perform plays and conduct worship. We create rich communication systems like American Sign Language.

Sending and Receiving "Texts"

The most common word for the basic unit of symbolic communication is "message." One simple word can be a powerful message: "Stop!" So can one image, such as a cross—meaning that Jesus died and has risen.

Communication scholars use the word "text" to refer to every type of message. Texts are not just written words. Texts are meaningful units of verbal or nonverbal symbols. Our clothing is a nonverbal text. A selfie is a text. A gorgeous sunset can be a text, declaring the glory of God (Ps. 19:1). Poet Mary Oliver writes that "each pond with its blazing lilies / is a prayer heard and answered lavishly."[7]

As we communicate, we exchange one another's texts. We share messages, hoping that our *interpretations* (understandings) are similar; we seek to know what texts mean. Complicated texts rarely mean exactly the same thing to two persons, let alone everyone. A word like "sin" can mean different things to different people, quite apart from how it is used in Scripture. Normally we interpret one another's texts without thinking much about the process of sending and receiving. When our messages are complicated, however, we might have to use additional texts, such as through conversations, to better explain our meaning.

Postmodern scholars say that sharing understanding is always problematic. They argue that no two people will ever completely understand the other's texts—and certainly not their intentions. Some of these scholars say that the best we can do is interpret texts for ourselves—what texts mean to us personally, not necessarily what they mean (or meant) to the sender or anyone else. In other words, just as message senders can creatively express meaning, receivers can creatively interpret messages. Shared understanding is problematic; no message means exactly the same thing to all people. The process of *encoding* (sending) and *decoding* (receiving) messages is *subjective*—based on imperfect human interpretation.

Postmodernists have a point.[8] In a fallen world, communication is always somewhat problematic. Encoding and decoding messages is never perfect. Nevertheless, we humans

Toe-to-Toe Warnings

My wife and I have created our own verbal and nonverbal codes so we can quickly and privately communicate in various situations. Sometimes all it takes is a glance of our eyes to convey what we are thinking. When my wife touches me on the foot with her toes under the dining table at gatherings, I know it is time for me to pay special attention to what I am saying for fear of offending others. Her taps are unmistakable warnings—toe-to-toe message alerts.

do create, interpret, and understand many messages. We work and play together using symbols. We come to understand what others mean, more or less, and certainly enough to care for God's world together. Postmodernists seem to overlook what a marvelous gift human communication really is—and how well we mere mortals can use the gift to serve God and one another.

Sharing Understanding

What exactly is communication? How do we know when it occurs? When two or more people share the same understanding (or interpretation) of the meaning of a message, communication occurs. Through the gift of communication, we create shared understanding. Successful communication is shared understanding of the meaning of symbols. Misunderstanding is the lack of mutual understanding; it is failed or at least insufficient communication.

My female acquaintance had to interpret the meaning of my comment about her friend's dress and legs. What did I mean? How should she understand me? She understood the

True or False?
"You Cannot Not Communicate"

A common saying about human communication is "You cannot not communicate."[a] It means that others will assess our message based on nonverbal cues along with our spoken words. We often interpret one another based on little real information. For instance, as soon as we stand up to give a speech, the audience will make assumptions about us based on our facial expressions, mannerisms, and attire. So we have to consider how others might perceive even our *cues*—unintended messages that can support or conflict with our intended messages.

Are audience assumptions necessarily communication? Not if we define communication as creating shared understanding. One-way interpretation of symbols is insufficient. For instance, the audience might read into an actor's nonverbals some messages that the actor is not intending to communicate. Actors spend years learning just how to walk on the stage or in front of a camera in order to subtly convey their characters' emotions. Great actors aim to make all of their verbal and nonverbal actions intentionally meaningful so that audiences can easily decode (interpret) and understand them.

a. The concept of "You cannot not communicate" was popularized by Paul Watzlawick as one of his five basic axioms for an "interactional view" of communication. See Paul Watzlawick, Janet Beavin Bavelas, and Don D. Jackson, *Pragmatics of Human Communication: A Study of Interactional Patterns, Pathologies, and Paradoxes* (New York: Norton, 2011), 30.

basic idea that I was asking her out to lunch, even though I got some of the facts wrong.

Contextualizing Communication

Thankfully, much of our communication creates immediate, shared understanding because it is simple and straightforward: "My name is Fernando."

Relational communication is more complicated because the *context*—the entire situation, including what was communicated previously—matters greatly. Asking someone out for a date is not so easy. What we say and how we say it can change how we are understood. Context includes the history of our relationship with each person. What does it mean if we ask someone to meet for coffee? Are we just trying to get to know the person better? Do we want to share a personal struggle with them and seek advice? Also, what exactly is a "date"?

What if we tell someone that we "like" them? How should we understand a compliment such as "You look great"? Such short messages can be relationally complicated and easily misunderstood, partly because of different contexts.

What does it mean when we say "I love you"? The meaning depends partly on the people and context. When we say it to an infant, it means something different from when we say it to a spouse on a wedding anniversary. No wonder understanding the Bible—which includes numerous cultural contexts—can be challenging.

We can easily offend when we misunderstand context. Augustine says that we should "pay careful attention to the conduct appropriate to different places, times, and persons, in case we make rash imputations of wickedness."[9] Being able to overcome such context-related confusion and offensiveness to gain shared understanding is truly worth giving thanks for.

Doing Communication

Communicating—creating shared understanding—is action. We do it together, just like playing video games or sports

Dressing for a Cross-Cultural Job Interview

Thinking about how to dress for a job interview creates anxiety. We wonder what we should wear—trying to determine what our interviewers might expect. We also wonder what will make us appear properly professional. Even "business casual" means different things to different people in different types of organizations and in different geographic areas. If we are going to dress for a job that involves cross-cultural work, chances are we will be evaluated significantly based on our apparent sensitivity to others' expectations. Our interviewers will wonder whether we are culturally sensitive, particularly for high-context cultures where dress needs to be finely tuned to circumstances and events.[a] In other words, we need to become intentional about what our clothing might unintentionally "say" to our audience.

a. On the differences between high- and low-context culture, see James E. Plueddemann, *Teaching across Cultures: Contextualizing Education for Global Mission* (Downers Grove, IL: IVP Academic, 2018), 60.

with one another. A rich understanding of one another does not happen passively; we have to work at it.

One of the most common Hebrew words for speech, *dabar*, suggests action or doing.[10] We accomplish things with words. We promise, warn, declare, threaten, and encourage.[11] We teach and learn. All of our relational activities depend on our ability to actively create shared understanding.

For instance, our best listening occurs when we actively use our hearts and minds to understand others. *Passive listening*—not actively considering what someone means—lacks attentiveness; it is more like daydreaming than real communication. Author Adam McHugh says we need listening hearts in order to grow relationally. He says that when the Lord asked King Solomon what he wanted, Solomon

> ### Start a Gratitude Board
>
> One way I nurture gratitude in my heart is by keeping track of things for which I am thankful. I use a corkboard on a wall at home so I see it regularly. I post reminders of blessings in my life. They include photographs (one of my baptism), ticket stubs, handwritten notes from friends and coworkers, Bible verses, emails, text messages, and a prayer that my mother kept in an envelope in her dresser.

asked for a "listening heart."[12] Communication professor Mary Darling says that "active soul listening" includes listening "to possible meanings that may lie beyond the actual spoken words."[13]

The heartfelt action of communication is a wonderful gift. As I am writing these words, I am imagining readers both understanding me and putting the principles of servant communication into action. While writing, I am praying often, "Lord, please direct my work to open readers' hearts and minds in tune with your Spirit."

Understanding with Discernment

Of course, we should evaluate others' messages, not just understand them. Do others truly know what they are talking about? Should we believe the media, politicians, and management?

We naturally ask such questions because of the gift of *discernment*—the ability to critically evaluate messages. In addition to understanding others, we can say "yes" or "no" to their messages. Our shared symbols depend on this human capacity for the negative.[14] We do not have to agree with everyone, let alone do what they say we should do. Discernment requires understanding and critical evaluation, not compliance or even agreement.

During our courtship, my future wife and I discussed our feelings toward each other. We sought to create a shared understanding of our relationship. Were we really in love? Was God blessing our relationship? Should we consider marriage? These were topics for shared discernment. We were actively defining the meaning of our relationship—saying "yes" or "no" to different understandings. At our wedding, we both said "Yes!" We thanked God for the promises we made to each other.

Conclusion

As soon as I made the inappropriate and erroneous compliment about the yellow dress and lovely legs, I figured I was in trouble. I felt like my emotions had run wildly ahead of my mind. Fortunately, my female acquaintance glimpsed the goodness in my heart. We laughed and agreed to meet for lunch.

Over four decades later, I can see the work of God in my awkward request and her kind acceptance. I am grateful. And my wife has a wonderful story to tell about her husband, a communication professor, who fumbled his attempt to ask her out but still eventually wed her.

I encourage you to prayerfully consider the gift of communication in your own life. Regularly give thanks to God for it. It will fill your heart so you can become a grateful servant communicator.

FOR DISCUSSION

1. What can we do daily to make us more grateful communicators? What keeps us from doing it?

2. When are you most likely to engage in metacommunication—communication about communication? Why?

3. Why do you think that the cross has become the most universal visual symbol for Christianity? Why not the fish symbol, which was used in the early church?

4. Can we ever fully understand one another and God? Even if we cannot, should it make any difference for how carefully we try to communicate?

5. Do you agree with the idea that you cannot *not* communicate? If so, how do you define communication?

3

Be Responsible

So the man gave names to all the livestock, the
birds in the sky and all the wild animals.

—Genesis 2:20

During my senior year in college, I started a job in radio advertising. I liked the people, the music, the challenge of selling radio time, and the fun of writing copy. Before I decided to go to graduate school, it was the kind of career that I could see myself in for many years. But then something totally unexpected happened that shook my confidence.

The station owner directed me to write short radio ads for a local company. "What company?" I asked. He gave me the name of a massage parlor. I said, "Is it a legitimate place? Do they do real massages?" He laughed and said,

"Whaddya think, kid?" The station manager confirmed that the place sold sex. He also said that we had to run the ads because the salesman, who had recently been fired, traded radio time for "massages," and we owed the business radio time and advertising copy. I wondered, as a new follower of Jesus Christ, what I should do. Later in the chapter, I will explain what I did.

This chapter addresses our responsibility to communicate under God's authority, in Jesus's name. We are servant communicators called to use the gift of communication to love God and our neighbors as ourselves.

Communicating Responsibly in God's Name

God's first general task for humans was to be fruitful, multiply, and have dominion over creation—what is sometimes called the "cultural mandate."[1] As Abraham Heschel puts it, what Adam heard first was a command.[2] But the first specific task was for Adam to name the animals (Gen. 2:20).

In ancient Hebrew, naming was a kind of "accounting" that indicated both identity (*what* something was) and ownership (*whose* it was). In a sense, Adam gave an accounting of the creatures that God had created. This kind of name-accounting is crucially important in Scripture. It can be traced all the way to the book of Revelation, which names those in the "book of life" who will dwell and reign with Christ (Rev. 3:5; 20:12, 15; cf. Phil. 4:3).

So we might imagine Adam's "naming" as something like this: "This is a pig—God's pig, which I am taking care of on his behalf." Adam, like us, was a caretaker of God's world, gifted with language to do his work responsibly under God's authority (in God's account and according to Adam's faithful accounting). In effect, God is our king and we are his special linguistic workers. We are called to communicate responsibly in God's name, not just in our own names for our own earthly purposes. Heschel says that we have a sense of "indebtedness," of "having a task and being called."[3]

In Scripture, we humans are seen as one of God's most distinct creaturely species, made in the image and likeness of God with a special responsibility to serve our Creator (Gen. 1:27–28). Humans are caretakers of the Creator's world.[4] Language equips us to hear God's call, communicate with God, and learn with the help of Scripture and the Holy Spirit to be accountable to him. We all are accountable to God—not just to others and ourselves—for our communication.

In other words, language involves personal and shared responsibility, not just using symbols and sharing messages.

Communication as Prayer

Our responsibility to use the gift of language with mindfulness that we are caretakers of God's world is so all-encompassing that we might even view our everyday communication as prayer. Paul says that we should pray without ceasing (1 Thess. 5:16).

Suppose we silently conclude every one of our messages this way: "In the name of the Father, Son, and Holy Spirit." Each of our texts, emails, and photo postings are part of the all-encompassing, lifelong responsibility we inherit as God's communicators. We are not our own linguistic masters, since all symbols belong to God. How might this change how we communicate?

Biblically speaking, we humans do not ultimately own anything, including language. God gives us language to use on his behalf and in the service of him and others. We are called to communicate responsibly in the name of God, who holds us accountable.

Listening Obediently

From a biblical perspective, human listening means both understanding and obeying.[5] When Jesus commands us to listen, he is not just asking us to understand him; he is calling us and telling us what we should do. Jesus's words are meant to be taken to heart and followed.

In fact, ancient Hebrew has no word for what we think of in English as "obey." One of the main words translated as "obey" in the Old Testament is *shema*, which literally means "listen," as in to hear, heed, understand, and then do. *Shema* is often translated simply as "hear." The Shema itself, for example—a daily Jewish prayer taken from Deuteronomy 6:4–9—begins, "Hear, O Israel, the LORD our God, the LORD is one" (v. 4).

Proverbs further captures this connection between listening and doing: "Whoever heeds discipline shows the way to life, but whoever ignores correction leads others astray" (10:17). In other words, listening is not just about hearing; it has to do with properly understanding (especially God) in order to do what is right. Real listening makes us humble and obedient.

Moreover, our understanding has to come from our hearts—*shema levot*. We can understand something intellectually, but not necessarily in our hearts. Purely conceptual understanding will not itself transform us into servant communicators. Obedient listening involves inviting God into our hearts so we desire to love him and our neighbors as ourselves.

Listening Intimately

The ancient Hebrew understanding of listening suggests both obedience and intimacy. By listening, we can become intimate with reality—with the way things really are, not just the way we think they are.

According to Scripture, listening is attending to reality intimately. For example, listening equips us to know others as distinct persons. We can live less by stereotypes and more by knowing persons individually. Heschel says, "No two human beings are alike. A major mode of being human is uniqueness. Every human being has something to say, to think, or to do which is unprecedented."[6]

The ancient Hebrew term for intimate knowing is *yada* (e.g., Gen. 4:1, 17, 25). *Yada* refers to all close knowing, such as a "righteous" farmer's knowledge of what his animals truly need (Prov. 12:10). A wise farmer knows how to care for particular creatures, being accountable to God for the animals' well-being.

So we listen to others partly to learn how we can serve them. For instance, we use social media to stay informed about our friends and family—not just because we like following the latest news or enjoy expressing ourselves. We listen partly to serve others, to discover what we need to know so we can communicate on their behalf.

If we hear that a friend is particularly troubled and needs encouragement, we might ask other friends who know that person to help us understand the situation. If we will be giving a speech, we can listen to representatives of our audience to determine how best to serve them. If we are tasked with writing a report, we need to know who will be reading it and what they expect. If we are making a video, we can determine how it will serve a particular audience. We first listen in order to know both *whom* we serve and *how* to serve them.

As servant communicators, we are especially attentive to opportunities to use the gift of communication to serve our neighbors—those in need. My radio station boss was one of my neighbors, as were station listeners and advertisers. We act like the Good Samaritan, who helped the man who was beaten, robbed, and left to die along the road (Luke 10:30–35). We cannot serve others abstractly. Our serving—our love in action—has to be particular. Whom will we be serving? What are their individual or group needs? The best listening equips us to know our audiences as specific neighbors in need.

For instance, I need to serve my wife. I have to learn when and how to listen to her. And I need to know when to speak up and when to remain silent. I learn such skills over time, partly by making mistakes and partly by asking for and listening to her feedback. As I become more relationally intimate with my wife, I can use the gift of communication more personally to serve her. I increasingly know what to say, when to say it, and how to say it. I learn which media to use in serving her in particular situations. She greatly values receiving special-occasion cards, so I search stores for the most fitting ones, sometimes even buying them months and years in advance if I discover a particularly appropriate one. When I know that she will be having a rough day at work, I text her a note of love and encouragement around lunchtime: "Dear, I am grateful for you. Thanks for being my wife and friend."

Listening Actively

Listening is a form of action. To do it well, we have to proactively engage our minds and hearts. If we assume that listening is passive—that mere hearing is understanding—we will communicate both superficially and ignorantly.

Communicating after My Son Died

Stephanie Bennett, Professor of Communication

Sometimes listening well is particularly difficult. After our son died unexpectedly in a car crash, my husband and I could hardly speak. But friends, family, and our faith community came alongside us, helping us to walk through the first horrifying weeks.

Such grief is awkward to face, especially when it's not your own. It is also excruciating, mostly inconsolable. It is fierce. Braving the raw, rocky sea of our grief, our community of faith held us tightly and looked us squarely in the eyes with the love and empathy that we desperately needed. Their compassion strengthened us. They surrounded us with practical acts of care, and despite the flight of words, the unspoken "conversations" greatly helped us walk on more solid ground. Their nonverbal communication spoke volumes.

In the quiet, in the tears, in the hugs—we were consoled. Friends spent many hours on details, helping us through the fog of the first week of our great loss. Others brought meals, sent flowers, or offered simple, heartfelt messages of affection and care. They listened well to our tears. Their support massaged our hearts and soothed our souls. God spoke through them in countless ways because they were brave enough to sit with us in the pain.

Researching as Listening

All communication research is essentially listening—getting to know reality. For example, a survey questionnaire can help us know people more accurately so we can communicate with them more effectively. Similarly, companies conduct exit interviews with departing employees to learn how to better serve current and future employees. Communication research is about gaining a better understanding of what communication is, how people do it, and how we can do it in a more competent manner.

If my wife and I do not sit down together regularly to listen to each other, we fall into misunderstandings and even arguments. We need to actively check in with each other. How are we feeling about each other and our relationship? What are our marital expectations? Are any resentments emerging? What is giving us joy and delight? What is dampening our spirits? The more actively we listen to one another, the greater our understanding of the good and bad in our relationship. Then we can better love each other.

Listening Dialogically

We tend to think of listening as one-way communication—as "receiving." We listen *to* others. Actually, we can better listen *with* others. Such listening is shared engagement. It is more like *dialogue* (two-way communication) than *monologue* (one-way communication).

During sixth grade, I met weekly with a counselor to discuss how I was coping while living alone with my schizophrenic mother. We chatted while playing board games. After a while, I trusted him enough to ask for advice about communicating with my mother. The more we listened to each other, the more I learned about my mother's condition and myself. He listened to my concerns. I listened to his advice. We dialogued.

Listening without dialogue is always problematic. We listen best when we ask others if we understand them and then consider their responses: "Here's what I'm hearing. Do I understand?" Real listening is not just taking turns sending messages; it includes actively confirming our understandings of one another.

Often, others can tell when we have ceased listening because we lose eye contact and attention and seem to be thinking about something else. I get embarrassed when I suddenly realize that I am not listening well and can no longer follow my conversation partner's train of thought. Sometimes I have the courage to admit that I was not paying attention and to ask them to repeat. But far too often I simply let the other person continue without truly understanding them.

Are We Wise or Foolish Communicators?

Foolish communicators do not listen closely before speaking. They understand reality—their audience, message, and themselves—only superficially, often just selfishly. They are quick to speak and slow to listen. By contrast, wise communicators are slow to speak and quick to listen (James 1:19). They know their audiences and messages. Talking or texting a lot can actually diminish our shared understanding by decreasing our listening time. Multitasking can reduce our communicative capacity.[a]

a. See "Multitasking Limits and Predictors," American Psychological Association, January 26, 2017, https://www.apa.org/pubs/highlights/peeps/issue-86.

Listening Vertically

Since we are accountable to God, we listen "vertically" to him, not just horizontally as we do with other persons. The psalmist says, "The fear of the LORD is the beginning of wisdom; all who follow his precepts have good understanding" (Ps. 111:10).[7] We listen to Scripture, including what it says about communication. We acknowledge the authority of God's Word compared with our words. We accept his absolute authority over our creaturely actions. We listen to everything God says at the keyhole of our hearts. Much prayer is listening *and* speaking. God knows us and answers even when we hear no words (Rom. 8:26). I do not fully understand this, yet I do experience it. Without ever hearing God's voice literally, I sometimes gain a sense of peaceful understanding as I meditate on relevant sections of God's Word or hear it explained in worship.

I struggled faithfully to hear God's wisdom for how I should respond to my boss's order for me to write the radio ads. I opened my heart to God, sharing how I felt—anxious, confused, even angry. I read Scripture with an eye for understanding.

We listen to God in order to become more intimate with him (to know him and his Word more deeply) and to learn how to live faithfully (Jer. 22:16). We devotedly identify and act on our responsibilities to him. Sometimes I am convicted of what I need to say—a specific word or message—that will demonstrate through me the love of Christ to others.

We also listen to God and God's Word so we know what to say to individuals and groups who are on the wrong path. We have a responsibility to warn others about the dangers ahead if they remain disobedient (Ezek. 3:16–21). Learning how to do this lovingly, however, is essential.

Communicating with Excellence and Compassion

How can we tell if we are using the gift of communication responsibly to serve others? Two essential criteria for servant communication are *excellence* and *compassion*.

First, we communicate excellently. We learn and use communication skills well. We might need relational or organizational skills, such as listening and speaking. We might need professional skills, such as conducting an interview or writing a memo. We might need technical skills, such as editing a video or designing a PowerPoint presentation. We might need to compose a press release or social-media advertisement. We might need research skills to explore a topic or audience. In all cases, we need to learn how to communicate excellently.

Second, we communicate compassionately. We communicate from our hearts, seeking the best for others. Our grateful attitude is neighborly love. Often this means we sympathize and empathize with others. We never communicate indifferently, as if others do not matter. Compassion even captures the idea of "suffering with" others by taking on their burdens. In all situations, we communicate with heartfelt compassion and technical skill.

Communicating "Christianly"

The combination of God-honoring excellence and compassion makes our communication "Christian." Like Jesus Christ, we communicate with skill and heart. We serve God with skill and heart as well.

Of course, there are many ways of defining "Christian communication." We could define it in terms of evangelism,

---

Adopt a Listening Partner

We all need trusted friends who will honestly evaluate our communication. I share drafts of my speeches and writings with friends who offer me great advice and save me from making mistakes. I also consult with them on personal communication.

I encourage you to identify at least one thoroughly trustworthy person with whom you can discuss your communication issues and opportunities. The goals are: (1) to understand each other, (2) to help each other evaluate past communication, and (3) to help each other address communication challenges with excellence and compassion.

---

a biblical worldview, specific biblical topics such as prayer and holiness, or serving Christian audiences such as church-goers. These definitions can be helpful, particularly if we combine excellence and compassion with each one. But often we use the phrase "Christian communication" without any precise meaning that would obligate us to serve God and others with both excellence and compassion. We just categorize messages and individuals, often stereotypically.

Embracing Confusion

Sometimes confusion is a good thing. I have created confusion intentionally in my desire to be responsible to God.

I wrote confusing radio ads for the massage parlor. According to the station manager, someone had to write those ads because the station did not have the money to reimburse the massage parlor for services rendered. Either I could write the ads, as the station owner requested, or someone else might be willing to do it. I grappled with the ethical dilemma, eventually agreeing to write the copy. I composed meaningless radio ads. It was quite a challenge to put a lot of words on a page and make them sound like they made sense while actually saying nothing. When our on-air talents would read the ads, they chuckled. The commercials became a running joke at the station; everyone seemed to think the ads were clever.

I cannot say that I did the right thing. But I am comforted by the fact that those commercials probably did not entice anyone to go to the massage parlor. And apparently those who worked at the parlor did not listen to our station, because we never received complaints. Obviously, I did not serve the interests of that particular business. Was I wrong? Maybe so. I wonder what I would to today if I were in the same situation.

We generally assume that we are above-average communicators, so we tend to get lazy. Unless conflicts arise, we keep communicating as usual. In effect, we do not hold ourselves accountable for excellent and compassionate communication until we get into trouble. Recognizing our own confusion can be a helpful sign that we need to do better.

Active listening—even to ourselves—often increases our confusion at first. In fact, confusion can be a sign that we are listening well. We are challenging our assumptions so we can understand more fully.

I spent years in therapy, listening as well as sharing my feelings and experiences. Therapists helped me understand myself and my relationships with others. At first, my therapists' observations confused me. Sometimes my own comments confused me: "Why did I say that?" The more I listened to my therapist and asked for clarification, however, the more I understood myself and how others likely perceived my communication.

> ## Create Communication-Related Mission Statements
>
> I write communication-oriented mission statements for my projects and relationships. I use them to remind myself what I am doing and why I am doing it (my motives). For this book project, I wrote, "I will skillfully use relevant personal examples and biblical insights to compassionately help readers become grateful servant communicators."
>
> Consider writing a one-sentence, communication-focused mission statement for a person or group you currently feel called to serve—perhaps family, friends, classmates, coworkers, or a church group. In your own language, capture excellence and compassion. Post the statement where you will see it regularly to keep you accountable to yourself, maybe as a computer screensaver or phone image.
>
> Some of my students and artistic friends have taken this one step further, creating visual and musical mission statements. They have used poetry, watercolor, graphic art, and dance.

As servant communicators, we identify our confusion in order to reduce it. We listen, especially to people who give us honest feedback. We become personally accountable for our own confusing communication.

Conclusion

I knew that I should not write radio ads for a massage parlor. I needed to communicate responsibly as a servant communicator, not as a publicist for an illicit business. But I also wanted to serve the station, which was facing financial difficulties. And I figured that if I wrote the ads I could make them unintelligible, whereas other salespeople at the station might try to write understandable ads that could offend our listeners and potentially drive other advertisers away.

God gives us the remarkable ability to use language, but then holds us responsible for using it with excellence and compassion in his name. To call ourselves "Christians" is a major responsibility. Do we communicate responsibly enough to merit the name? If so, our communication is like a form of worship.

FOR DISCUSSION

1. What would you have done if instructed by your boss to write commercials for a place of prostitution? Do you think the author made a wise decision?

2. Does it really make sense to define listening as both understanding and obeying?

3. Some comedians use the expression "yada, yada, yada." How might that common expression relate to the ancient Hebrew understanding of listening as "knowing" reality? (Hint: What do comedians mean when they use the expression?)

4. How do you feel when someone closely listens to you, giving you their undivided attention? Why?

5. Suppose we examine any form of "Christian" communication (e.g., Christian TV or Christian movies) in terms of both excellence and compassion. Are we likely to find more or less excellence and compassion compared with "secular" forms of such communication?

4

Address Brokenness

When the woman saw that the fruit of the tree was good for food and pleasing to the eye, and also desirable for gaining wisdom, she took some and ate it. She also gave some to her husband, who was with her, and he ate it. Then the eyes of both of them were opened, and they realized they were naked; so they sewed fig leaves together and made coverings for themselves.

—Genesis 3:6–7

When I was about seven years old, my parents once again started screaming and punching each other. I tried to separate them, but they kept swinging right over me. I finally gave up and went to my bedroom. Crying uncontrollably, I got on my knees and prayed, "God, I can't take it anymore. Please give me a real family."

We all witness relational brokenness. Something goes wrong. People stop listening and start blaming one another. They fight verbally if not physically. We know this is not the way things are supposed to be. I knew it as a child.

This chapter considers our broken communication as part of human "fallenness." None of us can communicate perfectly, but we can address our brokenness as servant communicators.

Accepting Imperfection

If only we could communicate flawlessly! If only we could understand one another fully and respond lovingly in the midst of conflicts. The world would be a far better place. But communication takes time and effort. Even a couple married for decades is still learning how to avoid nasty arguments by communicating more proactively.[1]

As a child, I expected my parents to solve their problems and create a great marriage. After all, that was what I saw on TV shows like *Leave It to Beaver*. Maybe my parents could have taken a few steps toward a better marriage in spite of their psychological brokenness. They could have sought professional help, but they seemed to lack the will.

We might as well admit that perfect communication is impossible. We should try hard to understand each other, but flawless communication is unachievable. If we expect too much of others, we will become impatient and probably resentful. We are better off accepting each other's limitations and striving patiently for improvement.

Being Vulnerable

One of the reasons we misunderstand one another is that we tend to hide our true feelings. Often it is too painful to talk about them. Even when our hearts ache, we sometimes act like everything is fine. We dwell in our own lonely, hurting hearts. I wonder how long my parents hid the depths of their resentments toward each other before their feelings began exploding as verbal attacks.

After their fall into sin, Adam and Eve felt shame, hid in the garden, and covered up their nakedness. So God went to them to initiate dialogue (Gen. 3:8–19). God knew what they did, but apparently he wanted them to confess. In any case, we all stand naked before God with guilt and embarrassment.[2] This is also true for media professionals who regret some of their work. Years ago, the advertising executive who created the Marlboro Man told me how embarrassed he was about the success of the legendary advertising campaign.

When we hide our hearts from God and others, we live superficially. Sharing our feelings honestly and deeply makes us vulnerable; we might have to face our shame, and others might hurt us. But without being open, others will not get to know our hearts, and we will not experience deep love. God wants us to open up with him, others, and ourselves. Instead, we hide.

Although it can be difficult and even emotionally painful, we can become more *transparent*—expressing our real feelings. Transparency equips us to love, and love drives out fear, including the fear of being open with others.[3] We tend to be more transparent with those who love us unconditionally.

Sharing Appropriately

Learning when and how to be appropriately transparent with others is one of the most difficult communication practices. We all want true friends, but we fear being hurt through betrayal. The more we are transparent with others, the more easily they can take advantage of us. Social media have complicated transparency because they expand our communication networks among people we know from different contexts and with different levels of intimacy. We are uncertain as to how some of them will use our messages.

We know that we should always be situationally appropriate, but it is challenging for any of us to do that well. Even if we open our hearts at fitting times and places, and with the right people, we still might get hurt emotionally. For decades, I never discussed my difficult childhood with my students unless it seemed fitting in a private conversation with an individual student. My privacy was healthy. As I found deeper healing, however, I was able to be more transparent and vulnerable in the classroom and eventually in my public speaking and writing. I could not have written this book so transparently even a decade ago.

As I became more appropriately open with students, they became more transparent with me. They shared difficult communication situations in their lives. Sometimes they even let me use their dilemmas anonymously as examples in my teaching, public speaking, and writing. They also admitted to me their struggles with faith—their questions, doubts, and feelings that the church is irrelevant and hypocritical. They knew they could trust me to listen well and keep confidentiality without being judgmental.

As I learned about their lives, my students showed me that we all need friends in our lives with whom we can be deeply transparent. Such friends bless us and give our lives meaning. As John 15 makes clear, ultimately, Jesus is that kind of friend for each of us, and such friendship is both a gift and a calling from God. Friendship requires hospitality of the heart. As one monk puts it, "My rule is to practice the virtue of hospitality towards those who come to see me and send them home in peace."[4]

I had to learn to be appropriately vulnerable for different audiences. Classroom, church, and civic audiences require different degrees of transparency. Probably the most vulnerably transparent I have been was in a speech to a group of mental-health professionals. I knew I could be open with them about my broken past and my emotional wounds, including my lifelong depression and anxiety. Eventually, my vulnerability became a blessing to myself and others. I became a deeper and more compassionate communicator.

Saving a Life

As a new Christian in graduate school I befriended a classmate who was struggling emotionally. I invited him to my home for dinner. We laughed and cried together about the pressures of graduate school and our similarly broken family backgrounds. After we graduated, I lost track of him.

About twenty years later, I received a note from him thanking me for our college friendship. He said that he was lonely and suicidal when I invited him to dinner, and my simple openness and kindness probably saved his life. I was astonished. All I did was listen to his story and openly share mine. Sometimes even a small expression of kindness and encouragement can make a big difference in others' lives.

Sharing Healing

Sharing some of our deepest fears and concerns with others is important for mutual healing in a broken world. Many of us suffer inside. Our own transparency encourages others to be more open. Together, we overcome some of our fears and embarrassments and even find healing.

Consider addictions—to drugs, alcohol, pornography, and so on. Few people overcome addiction on their own. Often, they feel shame. So they let the addiction close them off from others. Counseling helps an addict open up to a professional. Twelve-step programs like Alcoholics Anonymous go further, encouraging addicts to share their stories with one another while appropriately protecting anonymity outside the group. They create safe spaces for heart-healing vulnerability.[5]

Is Alcoholics Anonymous like the Early Church?

After attending an open Alcoholics Anonymous (AA) meeting with an alcoholic friend, writer Philip Yancey asked him to name the one quality present in AA that was missing in today's churches. "Dependency," his friend said. "None of us can make it on our own—isn't that why Jesus came? Yet most church people give off a self-satisfied air of piety or superiority. I don't sense them consciously leaning on God or each other. An alcoholic who goes to church feels inferior and incomplete."[a]

The early church met secretly in homes and included people from different social classes and cultural backgrounds. These Christians depended on one another for support in a hostile world. In fact, the early church became defined partly by the willingness of believers to hold steadfastly to the faith and become martyrs.

a. Philip Yancey, *Church: Why Bother?* (Grand Rapids: Zondervan, 2015), 51.

Suicides often catch us by surprise. We wonder why we did not know how deeply someone was hurting. When I went through especially difficult periods of depression and anxiety, I sought help. But I remember how embarrassed I was to share my darkness, even with a therapist. I wanted to hide from others, rather than open up, because vulnerability was so scary. Still, I needed transparency for healing.

Identifying Our Biases

In addition to avoiding vulnerability by hiding, we protect ourselves by communicating with people who are like us. We become *tribal*—staying in our bubbles of like-minded people. Our tribes might be ethnic, racial, religious, socio-economic, or more generally cultural or geographical. We feel comfortable with those who are like us. But the more tribal we become, the less we question our assumptions. We put people, including ourselves, into simplistic categories so we do not have to address complexity or even consider that we might misunderstand others. Søren Kierkegaard writes, "The majority of the people are not so afraid of holding a wrong opinion, as they are of holding an opinion alone."[6]

Tribalism creates one of our greatest communication problems, *confirmation bias*—seeking and agreeing with messages that confirm what we already believe. For example, we might consume only news media that reinforce our existing assumptions. We tell one another particular things with which we already agree, often without ever questioning them.

In order to identify the biases that affect our communication, we have to risk listening to those who are not like us.

The Pharisees' Confirmation Bias

The tribalistic Pharisees had self-confirming biases about Jesus, whose teachings threatened their tidy religion. Jesus knew that most of them would not accept his messages about the kingdom of God. Sometimes he spoke in parables rather than using statements that the Pharisees could try to refute. Why argue with someone whose mind is closed? Perhaps Jesus's biggest threat to the Pharisees was his insistence that they examine their hearts rather than just their religious practices (e.g., Luke 5:22).

The Pharisee Nicodemus first visited Jesus at night, perhaps to determine if the pharisaical tribe's biases were wrong (John 3:1–21). Apparently, he listened to Jesus because he provided embalming spices and helped Joseph of Arimathea prepare Jesus's body for burial (John 19:39–42).

It can be scary and upsetting. We might not like what we discover about our biases.

Blaming Others

Because of our fallen nature, we tend to blame others for communication problems. Adam and Eve each refused to take responsibility for their sins (Gen. 3:11–13). Eve listened to and then blamed the serpent for her own disobedience. Adam listened to and then blamed Eve for his own disobedience. Blame can run so deep in our hearts that it seems like normal communication. This happened to my mutually blaming parents, who night after night repeated a pattern of criticism and complaint.

Blaming temporarily relieves our own guilt and shame, helping us to feel better about ourselves. So when communication problems occur, we are quick to accuse others rather than accept responsibility. This is especially true when we resent those who do not live up to our expectations. I believe that this is what happened to my parents over time.

In short, we tend to be self-righteous communicators. At our worst, we would just as soon blame others as understand them, building ourselves up at the expense of others. It never really works. "No one heals himself by wounding another," writes Ambrose of Milan (340–397).[7]

Releasing Control

Another sign of our broken communication is our desire to control other communicators, often out of fear of losing the control that we never really had in the first place. We like to tell others what to say, how to say it, and when to say it, especially if it directly involves us. We might even say to someone, "What I must hear from you is . . ." or "I need you to say . . ." Sometimes we demand an apology, as if we would then accept it as genuine.

When we feel threatened or even just disrespected, we want to change others' feelings toward us. We especially dislike what we perceive as being ignored, slighted, or unfairly criticized.

At times, my parents were kind to me. But when my father started drinking, verbal and nonverbal chaos ensued. I wanted to yell back at my parents, telling them what to say and what not to say. I wanted to control the chaos so much for so long that I acquired the ever-present desire to control others' communication. I have to fight within myself to accept, rather than control, others.

As controlling communicators, we tend to nag. When we identify someone else's communication problem, we might start drawing attention to it. Soon we become overly sensitive to the problem and begin generalizing: "Stop saying 'like, ya know' *all the time*." "I hate it when you *constantly* say . . ." "You *never* listen to me."

Ironically, those of us who are controlling communicators often have the same problem we criticize in others. My psychological need for control leads me to try to convince others to control their communication. I even think I can fix others' communication when, in reality, I cannot fully repair my own. I say and text things I know I should not, often feeling regret almost immediately. My controlling attitude leads others to feel like I do not respect them.

Our fallenness leads us to trust less in God and other people and instead more in ourselves. We think we are better off taking charge and influencing others. But as we gain control we might use it to dominate, rather than to serve, others. Robert K. Greenleaf, the founder of the modern servant

Potential Types of Verbal Abuse

The term "verbal abuse" can be confusing for at least two reasons: (1) people have varying concepts of what this means, and (2) it can represent so many different types of communication. Examples include:

- name-calling
- blaming
- judging
- criticizing
- demeaning
- threatening
- demanding
- insulting

leadership movement, says, "Much of the best communication, especially to the young, is oblique. To hammer on a point and say, 'This is it!' is often to lose it."[8]

My parents were verbally abusive with each other, often hurling horrible language back and forth. The more each of them tried to control their recurring arguments, the more they actually lost control over each other and their own tempers. When I was ten years old, they divorced. It was ugly.

Sinning by Omission

Our broken communication includes sins of *omission*, which occur when we should have listened or spoken but did not. Some sins of omission stem from fear and shame. Feeling shame, for example, we might ignore people to whom we have long owed an apology.

One of my first-semester students stopped communicating with his parents because he wanted independence. He told me his parents called or texted him almost daily for the first month of school, but he just ignored them. He felt like they were not treating him respectfully as a responsible adult. I wondered if, by asking me for advice, he was questioning his actions. I suggested that he might consider the situation from his parents' perspective. Also, I admitted to him that I worried about my children when they left for college.

Soon he contacted his parents to apologize and to let them know that he was doing well. They all agreed on a day and time for a short weekly call to stay in touch. The plan worked, because his parents got enough information during the weekly call that they did not worry excessively about him. Also, by keeping the calls relatively brief, he felt free to leave out details that might make him feel like his parents were prying into his personal life.

Sinning by Commission

Sins of *commission* involve saying what we should not have said. Even if we do not verbally abuse others, we might lie, gossip, or overpromise. Lacking neighbor love, we treat others in ways we would never want to be treated. The mathematician-philosopher Blaise Pascal (1623–1662) says that "if all men knew what each other said of the other, there would not be four friends in the world."[9]

As servant communicators, we treat others "as ourselves." Using the gift of *empathy*—seeing things from another's perspective—we consider what would best serve us if we were on the receiving end of our own messages. Would we want others to criticize us publicly or privately? Would we want to be forgiven and encouraged, perhaps even befriended? We might even decide that the best thing for others is simply for us to respect them by listening to them nonjudgmentally.

Lying—making a statement intended to deceive—is on God's own list of communication-related sins in the Ten Commandments: "You shall not give false testimony against your neighbor" (Exod. 20:16). We are vulnerable to lying because lies can boost our image and protect us from pain.

Václav Havel, who became the first president of the Czech Republic after the fall of communism in that country, describes the results of citizens no longer speaking honestly under dictators: "The worst thing is that we live in a contaminated moral environment. We fell morally ill because we got used to saying something different from what we thought."[10]

Listening beyond Our Tribes

We live amid considerable uncivil public discourse, especially about politics. People attack one another online, in person, and via traditional mass media. Sometimes they hide behind anonymity.

One response to public conflict is to stop listening to others. A second one is to listen to others selectively, in tune with our own biases. Neither response is servant communication.

A better response is intentionally listening to people and media beyond our own tribes. For example, we can listen to broadcasts and podcasts preferred by people whose political views differ from our own. Then we might at least come to understand others and even discover errors in our political assumptions.

Another common communication-related sin of commission is *overpromising*—promising without a realistic, self-sacrificial commitment to keeping specific promises. All of our relationships are based on trust, which we undermine when we break promises. Ethicist Lewis Smedes says that we need to learn to live the love that we promise.[11] Servant communicators take promises seriously as loving actions.

Confessing Regularly

The best antidote I have found for avoiding communication-related sins of omission and commission is regular confession to God. *Confession* is identifying, admitting, and repenting of our sins. It requires us to understand ourselves as God understands us in the light of his commandments. This is difficult but essential. It renews our hearts with humility and gratitude, and it is the means by which we appropriate forgiveness. Jesus forgives repentant sinners.

Regular, honest confession creates shared understanding between us and God. It requires listening both to God's Word and to our own words. Augustine says that when we fail to confess to God, we do not hide ourselves from God; rather, we hide God from ourselves.[12] The more we sincerely confess our sins, the better our communication. Confession makes us more aware of who we are, whose we are, how we are failing as servant communicators, and even how much God loves us. That awareness, in turn, helps keep us humble and focused on serving. Dietrich Bonhoeffer writes, "The mask you wear before men will do you no good before Him. He wants to see you as you are. He wants to be gracious to you."[13]

Perhaps our restless messaging is calling us to confessional solitude. If so, we have a rich opportunity to become pilgrims who journey into solitude and, by doing so, rediscover themselves as God's special, forgiven children. We can pray something like this: "Lord, forgive me, a sinner, so that I may gratefully glorify you with my words today."

Conclusion

My father passed away when I was in high school. I both loved and hated him. I wish he had modeled good communication for me; instead, he demonstrated his brokenness.

When I was sixty-three years old, the same age he was when he died, I read a letter to him, out loud, at his grave. I confessed my anger toward him. I forgave him for being an imperfect father. It was long overdue. Since that tear-drenched day, new recollections of my father's kindness toward me have replaced some of my painful memories.

We humans will never be perfect communicators. Like Adam and Eve, we fall into destructive communication habits—sins of omission and commission alike. Our recovery needs to be slow and steady, flowing from our hearts as we honestly confess to God and seek to serve him gratefully, one word at a time.

FOR DISCUSSION

1. What's the difference between accepting imperfection in our communication and being poor communicators?

2. Why do we sometimes act like everything is fine with us even when our hearts ache?

3. When is it appropriate to share a deep personal secret about our lives with someone else?

4. Why might members of self-help organizations such as Weight Watchers and Alcoholics Anonymous share more deeply about their personal lives than Christians typically do in the church?

5. When have you changed your opinion about people or organizations based on new information that challenged your existing assumptions? As you look back on that personal transformation, what do you think convinced you to change?

5

Embrace Community

> For just as each of us has one body with many
> members, and these members do not all have the
> same function, so in Christ we, though many,
> form one body, and each member belongs to all
> the others.
>
> —Romans 12:4–5

O n the night before my son's wedding, he came to my hotel room and invited me to go for a walk. I was delighted. We strolled through downtown Charleston, South Carolina.

He said, "Dad, so what was it like for you the night before you married Mom?"

I replied, "I was scared. Given my dysfunctional family background, I didn't know if I could be a good husband and parent."

He said, "Dad, I don't feel the same way. You and Mom did a great job raising me. I'm really looking forward to being a husband and hopefully a father." I felt deeply grateful to God for giving me the loving family that I had longed for as a child.

This chapter explores our ability to form relationships through communication. Perhaps our best relationships are a taste of God's own community in the Trinity—Father, Son, and Holy Spirit. Maybe our most meaningful community life is even a taste of heaven on earth. Created in the image and likeness of our triune God, we are meant to dwell in life-giving communities of shalom.

Growing Together

Loneliness is miserable. Some individuals feel so lonely eating by themselves that they go to restaurants just to be near people. Others watch television or use social media while eating alone. The United Kingdom launched a "loneliness strategy" led by a "Minister of Loneliness." Calling loneliness one of the "greatest health challenges," the official government press release said that "up to a fifth of UK adults feel lonely most or all of the time."[1]

I grew up in a setting that gave me a taste of such loneliness. I felt abandoned by my parents. I often cried myself to sleep. My loneliness was so overwhelming that I still feel it when I recall those dismal days.

Life is most satisfying when we experience it with others. Many of our fondest memories are shared events, not lone activities. Our hearts tell us that we need to relate to others even though we fear vulnerability.

Communicating as "We"

One of the most amazing things about human communication is being able to speak together as a "we." Every organization we join and every group we participate in has a self-identity. Hobbies bring people together. So do political action groups, universities, and neighborhood associations. Families speak as a "we." Each "we" can add meaning to our lives.

The walk with my son the night before his wedding was a highlight of my life. His invitation and our conversation blessed my soul tremendously. We connected as father and son in a way that I would never have thought possible, given my own family background. My father died before I was married. My mother refused to attend my wedding. My relationship with my adult son is part of my familial community of joy, delight, and hope.

The words "communication" and "community" stem from the same Latin root, *communicatio*, which literally means "to make common." Historically, the term was even used to refer to "possession of a common faith."[2] Communication is how we create shared (common) lives. As we communicate, we form relationships that become our communities.

Knowing Ourselves in Community

Our involvement in communities shapes our *self-identity*—our sense of who we are. Through communication, we acquire shared values, beliefs, and attitudes. We learn how to act, including how to communicate. We learn a common language, culture, and faith.

When my son asked me to walk with him, he was inviting me to participate in a ritual of communication that we started when he was about five years old. We took neighborhood walks together after dinner, conversing along the way. The history of our walk-and-talk communion made his wedding-eve invitation particularly meaningful to me.

Communication can build up and tear down our familial communities. As a church elder, I visited families that nurtured healthy relationships across generations. But I also met with families torn apart by resentment and verbal abuse. I listened to the stories of adult children who had not communicated with their own parents for decades. All around us,

Identifying with a Negative Work Group

When I worked in a factory during high school, I took breaks with a small group of male coworkers. They criticized plant managers and gossiped about female workers. They rarely spoke positively of others, even members of our own group. The communication was like strings of one-line putdowns. One of the guys said I was so skinny that I was going to fall through my rear end and hang myself (he used spicier language). We all laughed, but he was implying that I was weak and unmanly.

As the kid in the group, I felt socially accepted, especially when I came up with creative criticisms that made everyone laugh. I received the attention that I never got at home. In a way, I felt loved.

As time went on, however, I grew uncomfortable with the group's attitudes, especially toward women. Also, our nasty language was making me a critical person—and I was enjoying it. So I began taking walks during some of the breaks. When I did join the group, I mostly listened. I accepted jokes aimed at me, but I did not reply in kind. I decided not to let my little work community shape my self-identity.

families are relationally growing and dying. My new family has given me a profoundly better self-identity.

Yet knowing ourselves also means that we understand our uniqueness. We can even communicate with ourselves about ourselves—called *intrapersonal communication.* As we communicate with others, we can use their observations about us to help us understand ourselves.

Nurturing Shalom

Our best communication nurtures what the Old Testament writers called *shalom*—right relations with God, others, and ourselves.[3] Shalom is the type of life-giving community we are called to build and enjoy together. It is a taste of what the New Testament calls the new heavens and the new earth (2 Pet. 3:13; Rev. 21:1). I tasted and then gave thanks for the shalom I experienced the night my son invited me to walk with him.

Servant communication nurtures shalom, whereas self-centered communication creates anti-shalom. Servant communication builds healthy community; self-centered communication breaks community. Every day we decide—explicitly and implicitly—to speak relational life or death. All of our communities—at work, home, church, and beyond—tend toward such shared life (shalom) or death (anti-shalom) (John 6:63; Acts 13:46).

Life-giving community is not easy to create. It requires a long, slow, shared obedience in the right direction—a steady love of God and others as self. True community cannot be formed just with scattered messages. Shalom requires a patient journey into the arms of mutual love, one conversation at a time.

Embracing Diversities

Healthy communities share common values and beliefs but also embrace rich diversity that includes both individual and cultural differences.

Each of us is a distinct person—body, mind, and heart. Even identical twins with similar DNA are unique persons. My wife and I had to learn how to raise two distinct children, just as they had to figure out how to communicate with contrasting parents. I was more of a vocal disciplinarian, while my wife was more of a patient listener.

I wrote on a university senior's paper that he was a talented writer. I encouraged him to continue developing his ability. My candid evaluation of his writing surprised him. He said that no one had ever mentioned the talent to him. He graduated a few months later and eventually became a professional writer and blogger. His particular strengths added to the diversity of talents in the organizations for which he worked.

Our cultural backgrounds can be resources for serving others. Each of our communities—such as our workplaces and churches—can be a source of diverse cultural experiences. Similarly valuable are experiences related to ethnic and linguistic differences.

The value of diversity is evident in our triune God—three distinct persons in one God. Each member of the Trinity knows and serves the other two persons. Their communication and community are perfect shalom in action. Perhaps such diversity within unity is part of what it means to be distinct persons collectively made in the image and likeness of God.

Diversity amid unity is the church's model. The New Testament letters explain how we should live together as distinct

> ### The Day My Church Ignored My Brother
>
> One of my brothers, who lives in rural California, stereotypically resembles a long-bearded hermit. When he first visited my West Michigan church, no one greeted him after the service. I am sure they were uncomfortable approaching someone who looked so different. As a result, they avoided interacting with an engaging person with remarkable life experiences.
>
> Stereotyping visitors is one of the most common problems in churches. Members tend to either ignore different-looking people or ask them questions based on stereotypes. Neither approach facilitates church growth. Instead, congregations can demonstrate their love for "strangers" (Heb. 13:2) by introducing themselves and starting general conversations.

persons in one body of Christ (e.g., 1 Cor. 12). God gives us different spiritual gifts and practical abilities. Yet we share one Lord and one faith. We experience some healthy tension between accepting different viewpoints and maintaining unity on essential matters like Jesus's divinity. Numerous Christian traditions have embraced variations of this, saying: "In essentials, unity; in doubtful matters, liberty; in all things, charity."[4]

Questioning Stereotypes

There are many ways of identifying human diversity, such as by race, gender, cultural backgrounds, and life experiences. Other types of diversity are less evident. Growing up with an alcoholic father and a schizophrenic mother was both a challenge and eventually a blessing for me. The experiences gave me a heart for students from difficult family backgrounds.

My understanding of such experiences is part of the diversity I can offer organizations.

We all tend to categorize people too quickly. We use *stereotypes*—simplistic categories that mask important differences among people. For instance, we tend to assume too much about others based on appearances and styles of communication. As a native, working-class Chicagoan, I learned to stereotype people who spoke with Southern (US) accents as less educated. Then in college I had a professor from the South whose slower-paced lectures and dry wit were an educational blessing; he was both a respectful and effective teacher. He unraveled my stereotype while teaching me much. Stereotypes deny complexity, whereas real-life experiences reveal complexity.

We all label; we cannot really live without labels because individuals and groups are more complicated than we can comprehend. When stereotypes take over, however, we lose some of the human capacity to build diverse communities of shalom. Some of the most relationally damaging stereotypes stem from people's appearances, from race and sex to dress and body image. We tend to judge others by their looks.

At its best, servant communication equips us to identify stereotypes and commune respectfully with distinct persons, groups, and cultures. In community, we humbly discuss and celebrate diversity. Such shalom is like the Trinity—diversity within unity. I do not fully understand it; but I try to avoid using simplistic categories for persons and groups. I know from experience that every individual has a deeper, richer life than any stereotypes can capture. Befriending even one person who is not like us can open our hearts and minds to individuals, groups, and cultures that we previously stereotyped.

How Words and More Can Bridge Cultures

Michael Longinow, Professor of Journalism

Words never tell the whole story. The communication we do begins inside and comes out of our eyes, our facial expressions, how we stand or sit. And people read us. We read them too. That reading gets harder when the culture is from another part of the world. And the wider world has come to our doorstep. Whether we live in a busy urban center or in a wind-swept rural tundra, there are people around us who have cultural origins different from our own. They are waiting for us to care about the culture from which they have come. When we ignore that culture, our words might be disregarded (because they are entering a space where they have felt unwelcome). When we take a step into that unfamiliar culture with a posture of humility and eagerness to learn, our words—backed by nonverbal communication—will get wings. We will gain awareness of cultural meanings we never imagined. It might feel awkward at first, but we shouldn't let that deter us. We must try it anyway: in a restaurant that serves food from another part of the world, in a plaza where the signs are in a language other than English, or in a worship service in another language. We listen to and beyond words.

Determining the actual differences in communication styles and topics among people is complicated. It includes differences in sex and gender. Some of our differences seem to be genetic; others seem to be learned. Yet we are all God's image bearers, even though we look and communicate differently. John Gottman, one of the foremost writers on communication and marriage, suggests that men and women are not radically different as people. Although gender differences may contribute to marital problems, they do not cause them.[5]

Male versus Female Communication?

My wife's extended family met annually on Thanksgiving Day. Women gathered in the kitchen to prepare dinner and converse. This was long before social media, and kitchen conversation was a way of catching up on family news.

The men met in the family room to watch football, occasionally commenting on the game and commercials. I was bored. I wondered if watching television was a way for the men to avoid transparent interpersonal communication.

After our children had fallen asleep in the back seats during the long ride home, my wife would fill me in on extended family news. She was my reporter.

I just went along with the Thanksgiving Day rituals, hoping each year to stimulate more family-room conversation. But watching football always won. Even as a communication scholar, I adopted stereotypes about my wife's family. We all deal with complex diversities by using simplistic categories—even when we know our own life defies stereotypes.

Nurturing Trust

Trust is essential for all of our communication. We need to know that we can depend on one another to speak the truth and keep promises. We begin to build trust when we listen respectfully to one another.

Servant communication nurtures such community trust. Self-serving communication erodes it. In a marriage, for instance, distrust can cut off communication, isolate spouses, and eventually lead to separation and divorce. When my son invited me to go for a walk on the eve of his wedding, we knew that we could trust each other heart-to-heart. We did not have to fear being open and honest.

Some of our most important communication involves promises and trust. For example, we might accept a job offer but then unexpectedly receive a better one from a different organization. What should we do? Should we ever break such a promise? If so, are we trustworthy?

Trust makes genuine community possible. This is simply the way we are; God calls and equips us to trust him and others for the sake of community.

The field of organizational communication has found that each organization creates its own culture. If leaders act differently than what they profess, employees lose trust. Management can send memos and conduct workshops to try to instill particular organizational values, such as openness and collaboration. If management seems untrustworthy, however, top-down messaging will not be effective; distrust sets the context for all communication.

When organizational leaders speak truthfully and keep promises, they promote a healthy culture with less fear, uncertainty, and *posturing*—communication intended merely to impress or mislead. Trust is a kind of social capital with

Distrust in the Workplace

I visited the office of a friend who works for a large, bureaucratic organization. Posted on the wall in an open area were notices from management. My friend and his colleagues wrote comments on them, pointing out items that were contradictory, incoherent, false, and even ridiculous. When I asked my friend about possible repercussions for posting messages critical of management, he said, "Nobody cares. Everyone knows that management is incompetent." I wondered if management agreed.

considerable organizational value. We nurture it by speaking truth and keeping promises.

Seeking Truth Together

Lying undermines relationships. When we tell a lie, we no longer treat others respectfully as equal persons; lies are abuses of power.[6] Augustine says that everyone who lies commits injustice.[7] None of us can hide all of our lies forever. Eventually others will discover some of them. Meanwhile, God already knows our deceptive hearts and actions.

As I mentioned earlier, a *lie* is a statement intended to deceive.[8] In order to lie, we have to know that what we are saying is false. If we text a message that we later discover is factually incorrect, we did not lie. We misinformed. Usually others will forgive us for misinforming them if we explain what happened—the sooner the better.

In the field of public relations, professional communicators represent organizations to their stakeholders, such as the general public, employees, stockholders, and the government. They issue press releases in hopes of gaining positive media coverage. They launch social-media campaigns designed to create positive public images. Sometimes they write speeches for management.

When stakeholders discover management distributing false messages, such as misleading financial reports or deceptive explanations for company layoffs, stakeholders lose trust in management and sometimes the entire organization. Stakeholders wonder if they can trust anything that the organization officially says. Communication professionals then have to rebuild trust by crafting explanations and apologies. Some public-relations experts specialize in *crisis communication* (defending an organization's or individual's reputation when it is publicly challenged) and *damage control* (measures taken to minimize reputation damage, such as proactive media interviews).

In politics, the communication specialty called "spin control" is designed to provide politicians and their surrogates with carefully crafted language ("talking points") to share

Promising to God in Order to Remain True to One Another

When couples wed, they usually make promises (vows) before God to love and serve each other. Some couples recite the vows on their anniversaries. In my experience, we are more likely to use the gift of communication to build healthy community when we promise to God that we will do so. Every time we start a new personal or professional relationship, we might promise to God that we will be servant communicators to those involved.

If we promise in prayer to God not to lie or cheat in particular kinds of tempting situations, and repeat the promise regularly, we are far less likely to fall into such practices. For instance, if we promise God to tell only the truth about ourselves to a new friend, we will most likely keep that promise without merely trying to create a positive image. Such promises apparently activate our consciences, helping us to be true to God, others, and ourselves. We practice what communication scholars Bill Strom and Divine Agodzo call "covenantal communication"—communication based on a long-term commitment to the benefit of one another as God's image bearers.[a]

a. Bill Strom and Divine Agodzo, *More Than Talk: A Covenantal Approach to Everyday Communication*, 5th ed. (New York: Kendall Hunt, 2018), 15–30.

with the public and media. Spin-control companies give political organizations specific language to use when answering questions about current events. Politicians themselves become robotic, mouthing the phrases fed to their brains by talking-point writers who are experts at deflecting criticism and attacking opponents. Much of the arguing on television news shows is centered on dueling talking points created by spin-control artists.

As a result of so much public deception and manipulation, democratic community suffers. Citizens align themselves excessively with special interest groups and lose a sense of fairness and common ground. A nation becomes a mess of squabbling groups with little commitment to honest dialogue.

Forming Truth-Loving Communities

We all are tempted to bend the truth. We want people to admire us, so we exaggerate. Christians, too, say partly true things to impress others. A friend jokes that exaggeration is one of the gifts of the Spirit. Yet shalom requires some mutual commitment to truth-telling.

Juicy gossip is hard to keep secret, especially if it involves someone we dislike. Workplaces breed *hearsay*—second- and third-hand information that may be partial or inaccurate, without the larger context. We mistakenly think that we can build relationships with some coworkers by gossiping about others. It works for a while, usually with people who themselves are gossipers. In the long run, however, gossiping always includes marginally true statements without the larger context. When we gossip, others may assume we are untrustworthy, if not liars, and will avoid confiding in us. Community breaks down.

As servant communicators, we avoid lying by surrounding ourselves with truth-seeking, truth-promoting people. We form healthy relationships with those who are similarly committed. I can take a walk with my son and we feel free, in love, to discuss anything on our minds.

The apostle Paul tells the Ephesians to speak the truth in love for congregational community. We grow together to become part of a "mature body" under the love and lordship of Jesus Christ. Speaking the truth in love builds life-giving relationships (Eph. 4:15).

Challenging Our First Impressions

We all assume that we reject stereotypes and appreciate human diversity. One way to determine if we truly value an individual is to challenge our first impressions.

When we meet someone, we can immediately ask ourselves what we are assuming. What do we feel about the person's looks? Manner of speech? Eye contact? The strength of a handshake? What social categories do we seem to be using to stereotype the individual? For instance, what do we assume about the person's apparent race? What about a wheelchair? Facial disfiguration? Do stutters or tattoos affect our first impressions? What if the person smokes or uses rough language?

Then we can remind ourselves to sweep aside such categories and accept the person as a unique creation made in the image and likeness of God. Jesus, too, was a unique person, wrongly categorized as a false prophet and subsequently crucified. If we knew what he actually looked like, we probably would be shocked; it might deeply challenge our stereotypes.

Conclusion

As my son and I strolled on his wedding eve, I gave thanks to God for him and our relationship. I thought about the importance of communicative rituals for building even two-person communities in a world infected with conflict and distrust. Shalom is a shared gift.

We are designed to create community through communication. And our communities, in turn, shape our communication for good and bad, shalom and anti-shalom. Like our triune God, we reflect both diversity and unity. Each of us is part of a diverse world, called to use our unique communication talents and life experiences for the greater good.

FOR DISCUSSION

1. When do you use the word "we" to refer to yourself and others in your life? What does that say about the communities in your life?
2. Can spending time with negative people actually make us more negative? What about participating in social media with negative people?
3. What times or activities in your life seem to give you the deepest sense of shalom? How is communication involved?
4. If diversity ultimately comes down to differences among all individuals, should we ever use categories to describe others? If so, what kinds of categories are helpful for us to communicate better with others?
5. Whom do you most trust? Why?

6

Be Virtuous

But the fruit of the Spirit is love, joy, peace,
forbearance, kindness, goodness, faithfulness,
gentleness and self-control. Against such things
there is no law.

—Galatians 5:22–23

The week before I begin teaching a university course, I
send enrolled students an optional survey about how
I can best serve them as unique learners. One of my
questions is, "What have you most liked about your favorite
classes?"

In response, students comment mostly on their instructors' personal qualities. They appreciate teachers who are
fair, patient, and friendly—not necessarily easy. In short, students like teachers who respect and serve them. A teacher's

character matters greatly to them—even more than an instructors' educational expertise.

This chapter considers the communicative importance of virtuous character. When we are virtuous, others are more apt to like us, listen to us, and sometimes even imitate us. Also, we are much more inclined to respect and serve them. Servant communicators naturally demonstrate good character, especially as reflected in the fruit of the Spirit. Titus summarizes some of the signs of a virtuous communicator: "to slander no one, to be peaceable and considerate, and always to be gentle toward everyone" (Titus 3:2).

Being Genuine

The ancient Greek rhetoricians determined that one of the most important elements of persuasion is *ethos*—the audience's perceptions of a communicator's character.[1] The Greek word also means "habit," how one tends to communicate repeatedly and predictably. One aspect of ethos is *virtue*—intrinsically good qualities of character. Virtuous persons habitually display an authentic, positive ethos. As a result, others generally like and trust them.

My new students quickly get a sense of the kind of person I am. Am I patient? Open-minded? A generous listener? Most importantly, do I seem to honor, respect, and even like them?

Of course, we can fake our ethos. We can project a mere *persona*—a mask that hides what we are really like. We can create positive impressions about ourselves that do not match our actual attitudes toward others. We can even be *two-faced*—putting on different masks for different people. For example, we might treat someone like a dear friend and

102

Dating Fakes

My neighbor asked me to help her fix a computer problem. As she and I were reviewing installed programs to check for malicious software, I noticed an online dating app. She said, "Oh yeah. We can delete that. I met three guys in person. They turned out to be phonies. Online, they made it seem like they wanted long-term relationships. They really wanted sex. One even told me that he was married but his wife was okay with him playing around."

We all can project false images of ourselves, even in person, but it is much easier to do it through mediated communication. We can take dozens of selfies to get one that makes us look the best and then digitally enhance it. We can write bios that highlight alleged strengths, knowing that our claims will not be verified like listed experiences on a résumé submitted to a potential employer. We all are tempted to create mediated personas.

later gossip about them. Similarly, some TV program hosts portray themselves as kind persons on camera yet are otherwise nasty toward production staff.

Hollywood celebrities, corporate executives, and politicians often hire publicists to fabricate public personas. Such public figures hope to project a positive image regardless of what they are really like as persons. Virtue becomes their mask, not their heart. The more courageous publicists give their clients honest feedback.

Seeking Integrity

Throughout history, many rhetoricians believed that a speaker's ethos should reflect their inner heart. Orators were morally obligated to be worthy of an audience's trust, convincing listeners partly by being intrinsically good persons, not just by projecting a credible public image. For servant communicators, personal character is foundational.

With the rise of mass media—like radio and television, which send messages to large, anonymous audiences—message senders and receivers were increasingly distanced from one another, making it easier to fabricate positive personas that receivers could not verify. Mass media celebrities try to shield their personal lives from public scrutiny. But today social media promote gossip by publicizing allegedly accurate and often reputation-damaging information about mass-media producers and celebrities. Meanwhile, the *paparazzi*—paid gossip hounds—try to find high-profile people's moral indiscretions and sell the information and photos to gossip-oriented media. For good and for bad, public figures are more easily held accountable today.

Christian philosophers and theologians have long admired virtue. For instance, a just person would be more highly regarded than an unfair one. Virtues were seen as good character traits that spring from communicators' hearts and shape their actions. Virtuous teachers would honor students by being honorable persons themselves. Today, a virtuous advertising copywriter for Saturday-morning commercials might respect child audiences by not using deceptive tactics to promote toys and sugary cereals.

There are numerous communication-related Christian virtues, many of which are reflected in the fruit of the Spirit: joy, peace, patience (sometimes called "forbearance"), kindness, goodness, gentleness, and self-control (Gal. 5:22).[2] By God's grace, these qualities can form our inner character and shape our communication. "May these words of my mouth and this meditation of my heart be pleasing in your sight," says the psalmist (Ps. 19:14). Integrity is all about integrating our words with our hearts.

Being Joyful

We servant communicators joyfully serve others because we know that our knowledge, skills, and audiences are all gifts. Joy-shaped speech flows naturally from grateful hearts and gives us joy in return. "A person finds joy in giving an apt reply," says Proverbs (15:23).

We all prefer communicating with those who appreciate our company. We cannot fabricate a joyful spirit, although sometimes we have to go through the motions when our own lives are disheartening. If we sense that others find little joy communicating with us, we wonder if they truly like us.

But how can we be joyful communicators when we suffer from hurtful misunderstandings and relational brokenness? This is one of the mysteries of our faith. Even though we all, like Jesus, are "familiar with pain" (Isa. 53:3), God blesses us in the midst of our steadfastness (James 5:10–11). The Spirit dwells in us and cultivates joy regardless of our circumstances. The apostle Paul experienced joy during persecution, even in prison (2 Cor. 11:23–28). As we pay attention to the whispers of joy in our hearts, the whispers begin speaking ever more loudly. The Spirit amplifies joy. Regular worship especially creates a spiritual diet of joyfulness that shapes our communication. Students prefer teachers who joyfully serve them.

Singing in Our Hearts at Work

Over the years, some of my coworkers were a joy to be around. Our conversations were natural, open, and heartfelt. I tended to avoid spending time with other, less virtuous coworkers because conversation could be forced and awkward. I feared offending and getting into arguments. When I worked in joyless places, I wanted to quit no matter how much I liked the work itself. Joyless places are bleak; they stifle life-giving interactions. The opposite is a place where people want to make joyful noises to the Lord, even if silently (Ps. 100:1). What a blessing to be able to sing in our hearts at work.

Embracing Peace

Why do some people like to quarrel? Why do they repeatedly disagree with others? It has to do with the condition of their hearts. As James puts it, they battle within themselves (James 4:1).

We servant communicators instead promote relational harmony. We do not avoid all confrontation, but we realize that when and how we communicate is critically important for fostering true peace in which people can flourish. Such shalom is not just the absence of conflict but the presence of relational flourishing. A married couple can avoid quarrels yet be relationally unfulfilled.

Scripture calls us to promote peace by avoiding divisiveness (1 Cor. 1:10). A servant communicator internally adopts, externally lives, and naturally speaks the peace of Christ even amid conflict. Stephen, the first Christian martyr, was stoned to death despite his peaceful testimony on behalf of his murderers (Acts 7:54–60). Instead of returning evil for evil, he virtuously stayed true to his calling as a loving follower of Jesus.

Yet some people approach public discourse with a warlike attitude designed to belittle perceived enemies. Many radio and TV talk shows are verbal battles with participants repeatedly interrupting one another to land spoken punches. They focus more on rhetorical combat than peaceful dialogue. Social media rants expand and publicize the battles.

Peace Communication

Gerald Mast, Professor of Communication

While walking to church, my friends were accosted by a man with a gun demanding money. When they responded by inviting him to go to church with them, he ran away. While I was planning a campus event, a coworker kept reacting negatively to my emailed appeals for assistance. When I asked how his day was going before again requesting his help, he responded positively. These examples illustrate *peace communication*—symbolic practices of compassion that move people from negative conflict toward reconciliation.

In *Conflict without Casualties*, psychologist and organizational consultant Nate Regier defines conflict as "the gap between what we want and what we are experiencing."[a] If we want conflict to be a positive rather than a destructive force, Regier suggests we express shared responsibility for resolving the conflict through creative questions rather than defensive reactions. "Do you want to go to church with us?" and "How are things going for you today?" are ordinary examples of peace communication that can reduce conflict and restore relationships.

a. Nate Regier, *Conflict without Casualties: A Field Guide for Leading with Compassionate Accountability* (Oakland: Berrett-Koehler, 2017), 9.

Sometimes even soft-spoken and seemingly sincere communicators spread disharmony. The psalmist says that our speech can be "smooth as butter" even with "war" in our hearts and with words that are like "drawn swords" (Ps. 55:21). This kind of militant communication is meant to hurt opponents. Combative speech might help us win a few verbal skirmishes, but in the long run it creates disharmony.

Being Patient

Many of us tend to be restless, impatient, and even impulsive communicators. We have much to do, and we do not want to be distracted by others. We tend to communicate with others when it fits our own schedules, needs, and interests. We expect others to communicate with us quickly and clearly, without wasting our time. We especially dislike group projects and committee meetings. Søren Kierkegaard says that we can be "seized by the whirlwind of impatience to be understood immediately."[3]

Consequently, we do not take the time to relate patiently to others. We practice hasty, ill-considered communication. Proverbs warns that there is "more hope for a fool" than for a hasty speaker (29:20). We set our own priorities and goals and get frustrated when people get in our way. We live in a culture of perpetual impatience and frustration, causing many people to be irritable communicators. Patient communication is countercultural today.

Except in emergency situations, speed rarely improves communication. Hastiness frequently gets us into trouble. Failing to understand others adequately before responding, we come across dismissively, as if saying, "I don't have time for you." So students especially appreciate instructors who patiently help them understand.

In the New Testament, the word "servant" partly means "waiting upon"—like restaurant servers who wait on customers. We servant communicators set aside adequate time for understanding others and formulating our messages. The more important our communication, the more patient we need to be. For example, reconciling with a long-estranged friend is not an overnight process. It occurs one step at a time, word by word, listening as well as speaking, rather than by forcing our own desires on them. The process of communicating is just as important as the goal. Sometimes we even need to wait on God's timing (Matt. 10:19–20). We stay attentive to *kairos*—to the right time and place, perhaps a Spirit-led opportunity in God's long-term plan for us and his kingdom (Mark 1:15).

Much of our patience involves simply listening, rather than trying to speak our way into the future. When we know that someone else is waiting for us, we feel alive and worthy of attention. Even just the thought of someone waiting to

Patiently Being What We Say

Søren Kierkegaard writes, "Busyness, keeping up with others, hustling hither and yon, makes it almost impossible for an individual to form a heart, to become a responsible, alive self." He later adds, "It is absolutely unethical when one is so busy communicating that he forgets to be what he teaches."[a] Excessive busyness undermines our efforts to be servant communicators.

a. Søren Kierkegaard, *Provocations: Spiritual Writings of Kierkegaard*, ed. Charles E. Moore (Farmington, PA: Plough, 1999), 19, 350.

communicate with us sends a signal of love to our hearts. Henri Nouwen says that we are blessed even when we know that just one person is waiting for us.[4]

Being Kind

Augustine posted the following sentence in large letters on the wall in his room: "Here we do not speak evil of anyone."[5] It reminded him of God's presence and his own responsibilities as a kind communicator. Questioning others' character is itself a sign of unvirtuous character.

The apostle Paul writes, "Be kind and compassionate to one another, forgiving each other, just as in Christ God forgave you" (Eph. 4:32). Paul reveals the heart of kindness in our ultimate role model, Jesus Christ. We put on the mind and heart of our Lord before we speak or text.

We tend to communicate unkindly when we feel that others have treated us unkindly, when we are jealous, or when we resent those who fail to meet our expectations. Our hearts get so warped that we justify our unkindness by thinking that others deserve it.

Preaching Damnation at a Wedding

A non-Christian friend complained to me about a wedding he attended where the minister pleaded with attendees to accept Jesus or risk going to hell. Did the minister display kindness by preaching damnation at a celebratory event? Should he have presented the love of Christ differently—or not at all? I apologized to my friend for the minister's apparently inappropriate remarks.

Loving Customers as Neighbors

During high school I worked for a kind man who verbally encouraged everyone who entered his neighborhood store. Sometimes neighborhood visitors would stop in without even intending to buy anything. It seemed like they were lonely and just wanted to talk. I was uncomfortable with small talk, so I tended to ignore them.

But the owner encouraged staff to spend time with neighbors. He often joined the conversations so he could get to know each neighbor's name and interests. He affirmed the value of every person who entered his store. He listened to them and genuinely expressed his gratitude to them for stopping by—whether they purchased anything or not.

Kindness is essential in our everyday interactions. We experience kindness in genuine smiles, welcoming and encouraging words, patient listening, and friendly conversation.

As servant communicators, our verbal and nonverbal actions should convey sincere kindness toward others. Kindness honors all people as our neighbors. It also promotes *civility*—polite, respectful interactions.

Being Good

I grew up in a working-class neighborhood where people used rough language. Crude jokes were especially common; they were like a verbal art form composed of obscenity, profanity, and even perversity. Our joking was fun, even if morally questionable.

In the New Testament, the word "good" can mean both something of intrinsically good quality and something pleasing or beautiful. In the same way, a "good" speech can be said

Signaling the Professor

Anonymity can bring out the worst in us when driving. A tailgater held up his middle finger as he finally sped around me. Apparently, I was not going fast enough for him. It happened on a street near campus, and the car had a student parking sticker. I doubt the driver would have signaled the same message if he had recognized me as one of his professors.

to be both well-constructed and rightly pleasing; it appeals to the best in us. A good movie is both well-made and morally sound, pleasing us artistically and morally.

The moral aspect of communication seems obvious. But at times we feel like we want to vent, criticize, and demean others even if we do not express such feelings outwardly. Sometimes these feelings spill out of us as words or nonverbal signals. Paul writes, "Do not let any unwholesome talk come out of your mouths, but only what is helpful for building others up according to their needs, that it may benefit those who listen" (Eph. 4:29).

Online anonymity tempts us. We are more likely to be good communicators when we are known. A helpful rule is never to say anything online that we would not say in person. Communicating in no one's name—not even our own—is an invitation to be bad.

Being Gentle

Gentleness is vital for servant communicators. Paul appeals to the Corinthians "by the humility and gentleness of Christ" (2 Cor. 10:1). Yet there is also a kind of rhetorical power in gentle communication; it opens minds and hearts, like an invitation to dialogue. Likely referring to the persuasion of even a king, Proverbs declares that a "gentle tongue can break a bone" (Prov. 25:15). The counterintuitive point is that gentleness is more likely to persuade than bravado. Others, even the powerful, feel less fearful or defensive when we engage them gently.

A mild-mannered spirit is better than an overbearing one. Gentleness is a type of loving witness. Peter says that we should be prepared to give an answer to those who ask the reason for our hope—and to do so gently (1 Pet. 3:15). Paul encourages believers to make their gentleness evident to all (Phil. 4:5). I wonder how to do that in text messages and email; maybe it is as simple as avoiding harsh language.

The apostle Paul advises us to stay away from foolish controversies (2 Tim. 2:23). When we get emotional about

The Default-to-Fault Rule

One way to cultivate virtue is to assume that any conflict or miscommunication might be our own fault. When we feel the need to point out others' faults, our egos lead us astray. Instead, we can teach ourselves to default to our own faults, assuming that we might be at least part of the problem.

For instance, interpersonal conflict is rarely caused by only one side's communication. All relationships are a mix of complex motives and actions. Only character stereotypes found in mass media are purely good or bad, perfect heroes or villains. In everyday messy communication, humility is the Spirit's door to our hearts, opening us up to our own faults and prompting us to identify the goodness in others.

Some of us tend to be too critical of ourselves. We overly default to our own faults. Still, there is plenty of fault to go around.

controversies, we can become angry and pushy. We take a stand, forcefully defend it, and sometimes even verbally bully others to accept our view. Then others normally push back, escalating the controversy. Controversial communication breeds more controversial communication, usually until people tire of it. This is what occurs with the news, which is often a string of controversial stories in endless cycles. Augustine says that holiness makes us gentle so we do not "revel in controversy."[6]

Being Self-Controlled

Our tongues are restless, not easily tamed (James 3:3–8). They seem to have a will of their own, leading us to express things we later regret, especially while talking and texting. We have trouble activating the switch that controls our communication impulses.

Servant communicators practice communicative *self-control*—self-censorship of what, when, and how we express ourselves. Without self-control, we might say too much, violate others' privacy, belittle people, and twist the truth. We jump to judgment without first evaluating our messages.

Instead, we can *reflect*—think to ourselves—while communicating in order to conform our words to our faith. "Those who consider themselves religious and yet do not keep a tight rein on their tongues deceive themselves, and their religion is worthless," warns James (1:26). Self-control requires us to listen to thoughts as we communicate, editing ourselves as we hear the words developing in our hearts and minds before expressing them. Such self-controlled

Communicating Prayerfully

We can nurture virtue by communicating prayerfully. We remind ourselves, until it becomes a habit, that we are communicating before the face of God even when we are not speaking directly to God. Our personal and professional communication becomes prayerful, offered consciously in God's presence.

For years, I struggled with recurring negative thoughts about particular people. When I would see them, there was little room in my heart for love. My grudges were like infected wounds in my heart. I could not think of them positively. Only after I coached myself to see others through Jesus's compassionate eyes was I able to reduce the bad habit.

I now ask the Spirit to remind me daily of his presence in all of my communication. For instance, at the beginning of my daily writing, video producing, teaching, and conversing, I remind myself that I am communicating before the face of Jesus. I ask God to show me the way as I seek to serve my audiences. I know that I need more than data and information. I need insight and wisdom about myself, my topic, and my audience. I need to ask the right, honest, transparent questions. I need a sense of awe and wonder, openness and humility. In short, I need to live prayerfully.

communication proactively saves us grief, especially in social media.

An ancient Jewish teaching says that the human tongue is like an arrow (Pss. 57:4; 64:3). Rabbi Joseph Telushkin explains that "if a man unsheathes his sword to kill his friend, and his friend pleads with him and begs for mercy, the man may be mollified and return the sword to its scabbard." Once an arrow is shot, however, "it cannot be returned, no matter how much one wants to."[7] Without self-control, we may often wish we could return our arrows to our empty quivers.

Conclusion

I learned as a teacher that the Christian faith offers a wealth of wisdom about being a virtuous communicator. Students admire (and will work hard for) virtuous instructors far more than they prefer particular teaching techniques or grading schemes. Probably like most people in most cultures, they look up to those who are worth imitating.

As Paul puts it, we servant communicators are part of our message. Our inner character speaks intentionally and unintentionally. We become what Paul calls God's "letters," with our "text" written in our hearts and communicated through our character (2 Cor. 3:1–3).

FOR DISCUSSION

1. What do you most like about a favorite teacher or preacher? Would you like to be known for the same characteristics?

2. Would you ever go to a particular movie, watch a specific video series, or listen to music because you heard that the artists are virtuous people? If so, how does their virtue come through in their medium?

3. How can we tell that we are communicating like peacemakers? Can you think of a time when you used the gift of communication to promote peace?

4. Is it true that speed does not always improve our communication? If so, when should we intentionally communicate more slowly?

5. Why does anonymity tempt us to view, listen to, and express things that we know we should not—even though God is always present?

7

Tell Stories

Let the redeemed of the LORD tell their
 story—
 those he redeemed from the hand of the
 foe,
those he gathered from the lands,
 from east and west, from north and
 south.

—Psalm 107:2–3

I took students to Chicago to meet with a successful corporate-communication professional. She told them, "At college I was a theater major. I learned that I have to know my story, characters, setting, and script. Every day I help our executives tell our company's story to different stakeholders, including employees, stockholders, media, government, and the public. I write speeches, stage press conferences, and coach our executives. I do theater."

Stories are probably the most powerful form of communication. They attract and engage us. They inform and deceive us. They give our lives meaning. The biblical story tells us who we are (God's responsible image bearers), what is wrong with us (sin), who saved us (Jesus Christ), and how we should live (faithfulness).

This chapter addresses the nature and importance of storytelling. As servant communicators we critique, create, and tell stories.

How Stories Work

We use stories (also called "narratives") for all three of the classical purposes for communication—to teach, persuade, and delight. But stories are not like propositional statements that are simply true or false. They can be subtler and often more convincing than even statements of fact. Stories can touch hearts as well as change minds. They "invite understanding. Stories are pathways."[1]

For instance, like Jesus, we teach with *parables*—deceptively simple stories that get audiences thinking. Jesus used parables about everyday life to describe the kingdom of God. Such parabolic stories invite audiences into the narrative to consider what it might mean for them. For example, the parable of the self-righteous Pharisee and the tax collector gets us thinking about our own self-righteousness (Luke 18:9–14).

We also use stories to illustrate our messages. The opening story in this chapter illustrates the importance of storytelling in corporate communication. In job interviews, we can use our life stories to illustrate our job preparation. Each résumé item represents a short story. One of the best ways to prepare for a job interview is to practice telling the brief story behind each résumé entry, focusing on what we learned and accomplished.

We employ stories to engage audiences. For instance, we might begin a speech, essay, or blog post by sharing a captivating story. The Gospels engage partly because they are narratives. The book of Leviticus, filled with laws and commandments, is not equally engaging; much of its meaning comes from where it is located in the greater biblical story of God's people, who needed specifics about how to live faithfully under God's law.

We use stories to persuade others by touching their hearts. Stories can create audience empathy and sympathy. They can move people to compassion. Nonprofit organizations tell

How to Tell a Story Well

- *Build anticipation*. Help the audience wonder what will happen next without giving away the ending.
- *Surprise*. Provide something unexpected rather than just typical.
- *Personalize*. If fitting, tell your own story or someone else's story.
- *Portray character*. Describe and imitate the main characters so the audience can picture and hear them.
- *Establish a setting*. Capture a time and place with which the audience can identify.
- *Develop conflict*. Highlight the main character's problem or unmet desire (whatever needs to be solved to make the story complete).
- *Tell*. Let the story make your point without analyzing the meaning of the story along the way.

uplifting stories about people the organization successfully served, hoping to touch the hearts of potential donors and inspire them to give.

Well-told stories delight us. We love to be entertained with both fictional and true tales. We enjoy telling and hearing them in everyday conversations and sharing them at special events, such as wedding receptions and graduation ceremonies. Getting together with friends would not be nearly so enjoyable if we stopped sharing our life stories.

Communicating Indirectly

Storytelling demonstrates the power of *indirect communication*, which Benson Fraser defines as conveying "truth by way of story, narrative, and symbol."[2] When we hear a statement, we tend to think that we should agree or disagree: "Corporate communication is storytelling." True or false? Agree or disagree?

By contrast, if we hear or view a narrative, we tend to wonder. When the corporate communication professional told the story of how a degree in theater prepared her for her job, she got students thinking about how her story might apply to their own professional preparation.

Narratives can foster conversation. This is partly why we like discussing novels, movies, and television dramas. We can share our personal thoughts about the stories without having to reveal too much about our own life stories. Then, as appropriate, we can join others in more transparent conversation.

If we directly state that "God is merciful," others might agree or disagree. If we tell a story of God's mercy in our lives, however, people are more inclined to consider our message.

This is why, in evangelism, a personal testimony (story) is often more effective than a statement for initiating conversation.

As servant communicators, we determine when to use direct or indirect communication. Often one is more effective in particular situations. A debate requires direct, often bold assertions, backed by evidence. A conversation begs for stories, even if only *anecdotal*—that is, based on individual experience.

Effective public speakers usually combine illustrative stories with direct, propositional language. When I lead presentations on résumé writing, for instance, I tell stories of my mentees' successes and failures. After each story, I explain why the résumé-writing strategies worked or failed. I begin with indirect, anecdotal communication and then add a direct, general explanation of résumé-writing rules.

Capturing Metaphors

Stories can communicate as *metaphors*—symbolic comparisons between seemingly dissimilar things: "Public speaking is

Characteristics of a Well-Told Testimony

- *Honesty.* Tell your story as it happened, not as you would like others to believe it happened.
- *Humility.* Focus on God's grace rather than your own efforts toward salvation.
- *Brevity.* Describe only the main turning points in your spiritual story.
- *Wonder.* Let yourself be amazed at God's goodness in your life.
- *Love.* Speak as a compassionate friend.
- *Respect.* Let listeners respond as they wish, even not at all.

a nightmare." Anyone who suffers from speech apprehension immediately understands the nightmare connection. Telling a story about panicking while delivering a speech makes the comparison vivid.

Aristotle said that "the greatest thing by far is to be a master of metaphor . . . and it is also a sign of genius, since a good metaphor implies an intuitive perception of the similarity in dissimilars."[3] For metaphors to work well, however, they have to be relevant to the audience. If listeners do not fear public speaking or never have nightmares, the nightmare metaphor will not communicate as effectively.

The corporate-communication professional described how she learned that her work is theater, but the theatrical metaphor also helps us see how she conducts her work. It makes sense to anyone who understands basic theater, such as the communication majors who were present.

When we create and consume narratives, we almost always think metaphorically; we apply the meanings of stories to things not directly addressed in the stories. For example, a prison movie like *The Shawshank Redemption* can generate discussion not only about human injustice and freedom

A Child's Metaphor for Heaven

When my five-year-old grandson asked what heaven is like, I knew I needed a relevant metaphor based on his life experience. He would not understand an abstract, theological answer. I thought about the things in his life that are most enjoyable and relationally rich, like splashing in the neighborhood swimming pool with family and friends. "Heaven is kind of like being at the pool together," I said. "It is filled with play and love."

from incarceration, but also about God's justice and freedom from sin.

Jesus hooked listeners on parables. His metaphorical stories suggested what the kingdom of God is like without literally describing the kingdom. Similarly, the fiction of J. R. R. Tolkien (*The Lord of the Rings*) and C. S. Lewis (*The Space Trilogy* and *The Chronicles of Narnia*) addresses biblical themes metaphorically as allegories of the gospel. Their stories invite us to explore make-believe worlds that capture truth. They portray power, ego, and sacrifice without directly preaching sin and salvation.

Mapping Life

Stories are like maps of life ("map" is another metaphor). We use fictional narratives to help us find our way in real life. We share and discuss personal and media stories alike. In a sense, communicating about stories is like being with others in a vehicle, mapping and discussing together the destination and our experiences and the places along the way.

When we tell a story, we are navigational guides. We get to set the destination (the conclusion of the story) and describe the characters, locations, and events in the journey. As we tell stories, we invite others to imagine themselves as participants in, as well as observers of, our narratives.

As storytellers, we all use our experiences, knowledge, and imaginations to represent life. We say, "You'll never guess what happened to me yesterday" or "The craziest thing occurred at work today." Then we tell our tale, using verbal and nonverbal language to describe what happened.

Story Discussion Topics

- *Identity*—what the story says about who we are as human beings
- *Intimacy*—what the story says about how and why we form and deform relationships
- *Ethics*—what the story says about how and why we act rightly or wrongly
- *Faith*—what the story says about God and about peoples' relationships with God

The meanings (or messages) of stories are always somewhat *subjective*—dependent on how the audience interprets the narratives. Stories are "real" things—actual narratives created by someone—but they are also metaphorical maps of life. For instance, film scholar William D. Romanowski says that narrative movies are "imaginative maps of reality" that provide "outlooks" on life.[4]

Eat and Tell

To promote dinner conversation with my young family, I encouraged personal storytelling. I asked, "What happened today that was funny?" It worked. Our children were not worried about giving the "right" answers; they knew that my question was not designed to pry into their personal lives. We still share humorous anecdotes when we gather for family events. Such fellowship reduces our apprehensions about opening up to one another. Food and storytelling often go together. When we Christians gather for the Lord's Supper, we recall the true story of Jesus's life, death, and resurrection. We remember that the gospel narrative is our primary map for life.

When we discuss a movie with friends, we discover various understandings of what the film means. When we talk about what happened to us personally, we might suggest what we learned: "I'll never do that again at work" or "I never had so much fun at a wedding reception; it almost makes me want to get married."

Engaging Comedies and Tragedies

How stories conclude often frames the overall narrative message. Broadly speaking, there are two types of stories: comedy and tragedy. A *comedy* has a happy ending, whereas a *tragedy* has an unhappy ending. After the fall from grace in the Garden of Eden, the Bible is largely a tragedy until the death and resurrection of Jesus Christ; then it becomes a comedy for those who believe and a tragedy for those who do not, according to God's justice.[5] Of course, there are "comedic" moments along the way, such as Noah's provisions through the flood and Joseph's reunion with his brothers. God's grace appears here and there, awaiting full revelation in Jesus the Christ, who rises from the dead as an atoning sacrifice for our sins.

We need comedic stories to show us how to be neighbor-loving persons, and tragic ones to warn us about failing to love God and our neighbor as ourselves. Such fictional and nonfictional stories can inspire us to live rightly. Discussing them helps us learn virtue and create maps for good relationships.

Tragic tales show us what happens when we choose relational death over life. Tragic storytellers indirectly warn us not to be arrogant and unfaithful; they practice a kind of

Turning a Tragedy into a Comedy

A family-owned textile mill burned to the ground, leaving over three thousand workers unemployed. It was a real-life tragedy for the area. The virtuous seventy-one-year-old owner decided to rebuild. During the yearlong plant reconstruction, he continued his employees' benefits, kept many of the workers on the payroll for ninety days, and promised to restore their jobs as soon as possible. Then he kept his public promises. He and his family transformed an apparent tragedy into a shared comedy.

"prophetic rhetoric."[6] The Old Testament prophets, such as Jeremiah and Amos, warned God's people about the consequences of their unfaithful ways. They told the stories of Israel's blemished past and foreboding future.

Given a choice, we almost always select comedic over tragic stories. We want to be reassured that things work out for good in the end. Most television series, for example, are like secular mini-gospels with a powerful collective theme: all things work together for good for those who are good people.

Interpreting Stories through the Biblical Metanarrative

God equips us to use the Bible to interpret stories. We can view stories through the lens of the biblical story of creation, fall, redemption, and renewal. We can employ scriptural themes—such as sin, forgiveness, faith, and justice—to assess the messages in humanly created stories. In a sense, we use Scripture as a map to navigate other stories.

In other words, the Bible is our *metanarrative*—the overarching story that equips us to understand and critique other stories. Scripture is not just a collection of moral lessons but also the ultimate story of God and his people, from Genesis to Revelation. The Bible is our chief story. It serves as a map *of* life (*revealing* what life is like for us as fallen but redeemed children of God) and a map *for* life (*explaining* how we should live as followers of Jesus Christ).

Also, we can create stories that map life from the perspective of our biblical faith. We can use scriptural themes to help Christians and non-Christians alike map life for themselves. These story maps do not have to portray actual biblical characters and events—as does the movie *Jesus*, part of the evangelistic Jesus Project.[7] They can capture universal truths.

Good Stories Are Universal

Tom Carmody, Professor of Communication

Many "Christian" films are aimed at Christian audiences; they preach to the converted. Another option for Christian filmmakers is to create "pre-evangelistic" movies that serve as discussion starters. For instance, the story of *Les Misérables* (French for "The Miserable Ones") is based on an 1862 French novel that was adapted as a musical in 1985, and a film version of the musical was released in 2012. The tale is interwoven with themes of love, justice, revolution, and ultimately redemption.

The play has run continually over thirty years, been produced in forty-two countries, translated into more than twenty languages, and viewed by over sixty million people. This story taps into universal human longings, such as being loved, receiving forgiveness, experiencing justice, and ultimately finding redemption. The story works because it appeals to our innermost desires. It will long serve as a vehicle for discussing the deepest desires of human hearts.

Critiquing Media Mythologies

We tend to assume that entertainment media do not significantly influence us personally, even if they affect others. This assumption is probably true for individual entertainment products, such as particular YouTube videos or television shows. But popular culture endlessly repeats the same types of stories with similar themes, essentially teaching us what to believe and how to act. As two media critics put it, "It may be comforting to believe that flipping a switch or turning a dial allows independence and freedom of thought and action," but it is "impossible to turn off a whole culture!"[8]

Taken together, popular stories both reflect and deepen a culture's *mythology*—its story-based, religion-like set of values, beliefs, and practices. Popular stories as a whole represent a secular metanarrative that sometimes competes thematically with the biblical metanarrative. Since popular stories can conform us to the ways of the world, we can live holier lives by biblically critiquing them.

Such *media criticism* includes understanding as well as evaluating media content. Criticism does not mean simply judging and dismissing mediated stories. It requires giving an honest evaluation based on carefully interpreting a story.

Two important aspects of critiquing narratives are portrayal and point of view. We can critique a story based on *portrayal*—the way it depicts topics, such as sex, violence, and profanity. We can also critique a story's *point of view*—what it says about a topic. For instance, a story's point of view could celebrate or condemn violence. Similarly, two TV shows could portray the same prayer scene, but one story's overall point of view could suggest that prayer is effective and the other story could suggest that prayer is a waste of time.

Romantic comedies link physical attractiveness to loving relationships, just as advertisements teach us to consume our way to external attractiveness. These comedies also suggest through their point of view that life's problems can be solved through romantic coupling; they simplistically "romanticize" love as happy feelings. Scripture, however, says that we should seek pure hearts; external looks do not make a person good (1 Sam. 16:7). Biblically speaking, the desires of our hearts tell our deepest story.

The Bible is the story of what God has done in spite of human sin. Media stories, on the other hand, generally portray what humans can accomplish without God. Whereas the gospel focuses on God's power, popular tales often focus on human power, particularly with action heroes.

Yet popular stories often affirm biblical truths. They can capture goodness, kindness, and justice. Stories can help us personally identify some of our moral weaknesses. Christians who write and produce mainstream stories have opportunities to open audiences' hearts while entertaining them. Augustine famously said that all truth is God's truth—wherever it is found.[9]

Conclusion

The corporate-communication professional who majored in theater compellingly shared her story. She persuaded students indirectly by relating her personal experience rising to leadership in a major organization. In effect, she offered a testimony to the value of understanding professional communication as theater.

Created in the image and likeness of God, we are storied creatures. We use narratives to teach, persuade, and delight in all areas of life. Learning how to critique, create, and tell stories across media is important for being servant communicators in God's world.

FOR DISCUSSION

1. Is storytelling really the most effective form of human communication? If not, what other form of communication is more effective? If so, why don't we intentionally develop our storytelling skills?

2. What was the last movie you saw, book you read, or sermon you heard that used indirect communication? Did it increase or decrease your enjoyment of the story?

3. Which, if any, of the characteristics of a well-told story strike you as particularly important for today? Explain.

4. Do movies actually "map" life for us? Are they not just entertainment? How can we know?

5. Does it reduce the seriousness of the gospel to call it a "divine comedy"?

8

Discern Media

That same day Jesus went out of the house
and sat by the lake. Such large crowds gathered
around him that he got into a boat and sat in it,
while all the people stood on the shore. Then he
told them many things in parables, saying: "A
farmer went out to sow his seed."

—Matthew 13:1–3

When I accept offers to speak to groups, my hosts
usually ask me one question: "Will you need
technology?" What they really mean is: "Are
you going to use PowerPoint?" They seem a bit surprised
if I respond that I will not be projecting slides on a screen.
Then I add, "I am the medium." My hosts will frequently
then admit that they do not really like PowerPoint presentations anyway.

All human communication requires a *medium*—a channel of communication. Sometimes technological media can greatly enhance our message. I use PowerPoint when I can communicate my message more effectively with projected visuals. Similarly, I write blogs or produce audio and video messages when appropriate. But I do not assume that I can communicate more effectively just by using a particular technology, since it can detract from, just as much as it can contribute to, our communication.

This chapter explores communication technologies (media) as extensions of our God-given communication abilities. It explains what media are and how we servant communicators can use them appropriately (or "fittingly"). We have at least three basic options: rejecting, adapting, and creating technologies.

Communication versus Communications

In the field of communication studies, the word "communications" (with an *s*) often refers to communication through technology, such as through print (e.g., books and magazines) or digital media (e.g., podcasts and videocasts): "Television is a communications medium." Sometimes "communications" is used instead to refer to sending and receiving messages through any medium: "Did you have any communications with your family?" For the most part, the word "communication" (without the *s*) refers to the process of communicating, with or without technology. Even more confusing, some people use the word in the singular as a noun to refer to a message: "Did you receive the communication?" I try to keep it simple by using "communications" only for technologically mediated communication. It is easy to miscommunicate about communication(s)!

Defining Technology

Technologies are a combination of humanly created *things* (e.g., vehicles and phones) and their *uses* (e.g., transportation and communication). Vehicles enable us to meet with people in person for conversation, but we do not use them as communication technologies. We can use a smartphone to calculate numbers or view videos. We can use cameras to take pictures for our own reminiscence or to show others what is going on in our lives. In short, technological "things" equip us to do many things—communication included.

Communicating with Media Technologies

Communication technologies are the technologies we use primarily to communicate—to create shared understanding. We can use other physical things to communicate by turning them into symbols, but they are not primarily communication technologies. God instructed Jeremiah to smash a clay pot as a visual warning of what would happen to God's people if they continued to disobey him (Jer. 19:10). Yet the principal use of pottery is not communication.

In other words, communication technologies are primarily *media*—channels for communication. We use phones and screen projectors as media to convey messages. When I address a group, I have to decide which media will enhance my communication, including non-technological media. As I speak to groups, my body, especially my voice, is my primary medium. Marshall McLuhan said that communication technologies are "extensions" of human senses, particularly seeing and hearing beyond what we can see and hear in person.[1]

135

Jesus Broadcasts His Message

When Jesus sat down in the boat to address the crowds standing on the shore, he expanded his audience by creating a natural amphitheater. He told the parable of the sower, which depicts a farmer scattering (or "broadcasting") seed across the ground (Matt. 13:1–23). The word "broadcasting" is still used to describe planting seeds by tossing them freely, but the word also describes the transmission of radio and television signals across geographic space to large audiences. With his makeshift amphitheater, Jesus vocally broadcast his message from boat to shore. When his message took root in his listeners' hearts, spiritual growth began.

So one helpful way to think about communication technologies is whether they will improve on our non-technological communication media, primarily our bodies.

Elevating the Spoken Word

Although we tend to think that technological communication is more powerful than non-technological communication, the spoken word is usually the most potent medium because it is the closest to our createdness, especially when used *incarnately*—in person. Jesus was the Word of God incarnate, in the flesh. Others wrote down his words and passed them along to us. But since we have only his recorded words, we can hardly imagine what it must have been like to speak with Jesus in person. Philip Yancey says that we tend to assume Jesus looked like a member of our own culture.[2] Filmmakers have struggled to depict not only what Jesus might have looked like but also how he spoke. Written and spoken communication are different media.

The Old Testament comes out of the ancient Jews' *oral culture*—a way of life based primarily on speaking and listening in person without much written (literate) communication. In oral cultures, the spoken word carries knowledge from person to person and generation to generation. People in nonliterate cultures must rely extensively on memory and oral repetition to avoid forgetting important skills and knowledge, including history. Spoken words maintain oral culture since books are unavailable for storing and retrieving information. Poetic language and songs are enormously helpful, and scholars have identified some of the ways that Jews used such artistic means of oral communication to maintain their faith over many generations.[3]

As writing and reading became more widespread, scribes recorded spoken words in manuscripts and made copies for future generations. Hebrew scribes recorded God's actions and laws according to what had been passed along orally from earlier generations. Eventually the written word led to books and new "authorities"—authors. One result has been that those of us in highly literate cultures tend to believe authors (printed texts) more than speakers (spoken messages). Spoken words seem more authoritative when they are printed.

Understanding how media work is extremely important for servant communicators. In order to communicate, we need to know which media will be most effective, not just the fastest, least expensive, or most impressive.

Fitting Medium to Message

Communication technologies do not communicate all messages equally effectively. Each medium shapes messages differently. Chatting with a date in person is not the same as conversing on a video date. Delivering a speech online with a camera is different from giving one from an auditorium stage. Camera close-ups highlight a speaker's face; stages highlight a speaker's entire body.

All media have comparative advantages and disadvantages even for particular individuals. Reading an e-book is not the same communicative experience as reading a traditional printed book—especially for study. Some learners prefer e-books, but most like printed materials. Some people are visual learners. A friend teaches second languages to those who have difficulty learning them. She has found that a multimedia, multi-sensory approach is most effective, so she includes everything from singing to body movements; the goal is to get the whole person involved in learning.[4] We all are multimedia persons.

In other words, some media are better than others for sharing particular messages with particular people for particular purposes. As servant communicators, we aim for *fittingness*—fitting our message to an appropriate and presumably effective medium.[5] Would it be fitting to terminate employees via text message or email? Is the communicative purpose just to fire employees or also to serve them emotionally? Sometimes our resources and time are limited, so we have to use a less fitting medium. Even so, we do the best we can to match medium with message.

Why are we not more aware of using the most fitting medium in a given situation? One major reason is that we are creatures of habit. We communicate more ritualistically than creatively. Day after day, we communicate with many of the same people using the same media and technologies. We do not routinely consider alternative modes, such as whether we should text a message or speak it in person.

Is the Medium the Message?

Marshall McLuhan famously said, "The medium is the message."[a] He meant that communication technologies shape our messages and thereby even become part of our messages. In other words, both our message and our medium affect how others will understand us. I especially like this version of the saying, "The medium is the massage."[b] Each medium "massages" our messages and our relationships. Media shape how we feel about and react to messages. For example, friendship seems to be different in the age of social media, although we are only beginning to understand how and why.

a. Marshall McLuhan, *Understanding Media: The Extensions of Man* (1964; repr., Cambridge, MA: MIT Press, 1994), 12.
b. Marshall McLuhan and Quentin Fiore, *The Medium Is the Massage: An Inventory of Effects* (1967; repr., Berkeley: Ginko, 2001).

If possible, I offer thanks and encouragement to people in person with a smile and a handshake. But sometimes I am not able to get together with others for a while, and I still want to express my gratitude. In such cases, I handwrite a personal note, which is more fitting than sending an email, text message, or even calling others. Handwritten thank-you notes impact me so much that I keep every one of them in a special file drawer and review them when I am discouraged.

Rejecting Communication Technologies

When I was a university student, a professor asked my class if all communication technologies are inherently good. It seemed to me like a silly question with an obvious answer: "It depends on how we use the technologies. We determine if the technologies are used for good or bad communication."

Selecting a Fitting Medium

The basic rule for fitting a medium with a message is to use the medium that will best convey the main point within the limits of time and availability. It helps to imagine how we might interpret the message if we received it via different media.

- *Emotional messages.* Select the most dialogical, expressive, multi-sensory medium, such as meeting in person or talking via video or on the phone.
- *Immediate messages.* Use the medium that will most likely reach the recipient quickly, such as a text or email, adding a note that clarification will be forthcoming as needed.
- *Private messages.* Use a medium in which the message cannot be easily seen by or forwarded to others, especially by meeting in person or conversing by phone.
- *Mass messages* (to many people at once). Use a medium that will best communicate a standardized message to a large group, perhaps even a recorded audio or video message rather than only a text message.
- *Instructional messages.* Use media that match an instructional goal, such as demonstrating with video or in person, or providing written information with clear instructions.
- *Complicated messages.* Use written/printed media for precise wording and to give the recipient time to read and reread it for maximum comprehension. Add visuals as necessary.

In other words, I saw media as tools for conveying good or bad messages. People make communication good or bad, effective or ineffective, regardless of the technology.

But then the professor complicated the issue: "What if using some media interferes with using other ones? What if consuming mass media like television and radio weakens family communication?" The professor described the Amish, who generally reject such mass media, which they believe disrupt family and local community.

I love using new media. I got a personal networked computer and started using email long before most of my colleagues. When cell phones came along, I was an early adopter. Still, I realized that I was not being very *technologically discerning*—understanding and using different media wisely. My technological decisions were not very informed by my faith. I felt like I still had not learned adequately from the Amish example.

My instructor got me thinking about whether I should necessarily use particular communication technologies—and if so, when and how. I began thinking that maybe McLuhan was at least partly correct; the medium shapes the message. Moreover, the medium shapes our relationships; we create and change our relationships through different media. Speaking on the phone shapes our messages—and relationships— differently than communicating through printed books and online chats. Eventually, I even wondered about the difference between reading the Bible silently and reading it out loud personally or in a group. It seemed to me that some media are better for particular communicative purposes, and that media interact with one another in our lives. As a teacher, I even wondered how students best learn—lectures with or without PowerPoint and video, discussions, hands-on projects, group work, and so on.

In addition, as a new Christian I wanted to know if the Amish were just trying to be faithful. I personally did not want to give up radio and television, and certainly not the telephone (only wired back then). I increasingly realized, however, that communication technologies are social rather than merely personal. I discovered that some conservative Jewish and Christian groups live out a conviction that local community needs to be nurtured and sometimes even protected by avoiding excessive, frivolous, and offensive communication from the outside world. After all, we humans become like the people with whom we communicate; communication and community are inseparable. I wondered if all Christian groups should sometimes reject particular communication technologies for the sake of community.

After my wife and I had children, I could see that the Amish had a point. Television competed with us for our children's attention. Today, I see a similar phenomenon with

Amish and Phones

Collective negotiations over the use of telephones have ignited intense controversies in the Amish community since the beginning of the 20th century. In fact, a dispute over the role of the phone was the principal issue behind the 1920s division of the Amish church, wherein one-fifth of the membership broke away to form their own church.

Eventually, certain Amish communities accepted the telephone for its aid in summoning doctors and veterinarians, and in calling suppliers. But even these Amish did not allow the telephone into the home. Rather, they required that phones be used communally. Typically, a neighborhood of two or three extended families shares a telephone housed in a wooden shanty, located either at the intersection of several fields or at the end of a common lane. These structures look like small bus shelters or privies; indeed, some phones are in outhouses. Sometimes the telephone shanties have answering machines in them. (After all, who wants to wait in the privy on the off chance someone will call?)

This excerpt is from Howard Rheingold, "Look Who's Talking," Wired, January 1, 1999, https://www.wired.com/1999/01/amish/.

my five-year-old grandson, who sometimes prefers to watch YouTube rather than play with others.

Even when we have concerns about the possible effects of new media on our lives, we tend to adopt them like everyone else does. We become undiscerning copycats. In fact, we usually see new media as signs of progress. We naively idolize communication technologies as powerful relational and evangelistic tools irrespective of how we actually use them. As Abraham Heschel says, we humans are "endowed with an amazing degree of receptivity, conformity, and gullibility."[6]

Adapting Communication Technologies

Being a communication professor, parent, and Christian made me increasingly cautious about automatically adopting every new medium. So instead of undiscerningly imitating other users, I tried to consciously make decisions. I felt called to *adapt communication technologies*—to use them in ways that would help me meet worthy goals, especially relationships of shalom. I realized that we can adapt communication technologies according to their different strengths and weaknesses for particular communication purposes.

For instance, I initially jumped into new social media, but discovered that I was trying to communicate with too many people too superficially. My communication network was getting wide but shallow. So I reduced the number of people that I track and interact with on social media. I created a small group of extended family that I check in with every couple of days. If I have time, about twice a month I

143

review the postings by people outside my smaller network. Similarly, I decided to restrict most of my text messaging to the same smaller group.

Augustine says that we should love all people equally, but adds that we should especially consider those who are closest to us in terms of "place, time, or any other circumstances."[7] In other words, maybe we have special obligations to commit our time and attention to those who are closest to us, both geographically and emotionally. Of course, Augustine could not have imagined something like social media, which enable us to connect locally and distantly alike, at all hours of the day and on any day of the week.

Creating Communication Technologies

In addition to discerningly adapting new media for worthy purposes, we servant communicators can develop new technologies. We can provide ways for all people to nurture community, build businesses, grow congregations, participate in democratic self-government, and so much more. We can be proactive leaders.

Decades ago, I worked with the team that developed the online BibleGateway. We felt called to create a technology for searching, reading, and studying Scripture online. We were especially interested in making the Bible available in countries where it was banned or otherwise unavailable. We realized that opinion leaders and government officials even in authoritarian nations would soon have access to the internet for their own personal, if not official, use. So we created Bible software for the emerging World Wide Web, becoming the first group to publish the New International Version online.

> ## Creating and Using Video Games
>
> Communication scholar Kevin Schut, author of *Of Games and God: A Christian Exploration of Video Games,* calls Christians to enter the gaming industry. He highlights specific ways that Christians can be salt and light there. He admits that when he first started studying video gaming he was dismayed at what he found. But he became more optimistic as he dug deeper, discovering creative Christians throughout the industry who were making a positive difference.[a]
>
> a. Kevin Schut, *Of Games and God: A Christian Exploration of Video Games* (Grand Rapids: Brazos, 2013), 145–46.

Once we launched the site, we started receiving emails from around the globe thanking us.

Conclusion

When I started speaking regularly to groups about communication, I was excited about using technology. The overhead projector, now largely replaced by computer projection, seemed powerful. But my audiences quickly tired of looking at screens. I could hold their attention much more fully by handing out printed notes as needed and using my body, especially my voice, expressively. I adapted my use of media to my communication goals and audiences.

As a servant communicator, I still love using new technologies. Even as I limit my media usage in order to reserve in-person time for family, friends, and church, I do not want to be left behind in the race to use the latest media. I struggle, as we all do, to adapt technologies wisely without just rejecting them. I have learned that discernment involves making wise decisions about media, not just about messages.

FOR DISCUSSION

1. Discuss this proposition: "Use PowerPoint only if you have to."

2. How can the Bible be the "Word of God" when only a small part of it is God directly "speaking"?

3. What would be the best medium to use to apologize to someone if you could not meet them in person? Why?

4. Have you "rejected" any communication technology (including software)? Or at least greatly reduced your use of it? Explain.

5. Is there any communication-related industry that Christians should not enter? Why or why not?

Closing Thoughts

When I first spoke openly in chapel years ago about my rough childhood and lifelong depression and anxiety, I was relieved. I felt like I had become more honest and courageous by trusting in God as I told my story. I had no idea how God was planning to use me to serve him and others.

In his letter to the church at Ephesus, the apostle Paul writes, "For we are God's handiwork, created in Christ Jesus to do good works, which God prepared in advance for us to do" (Eph. 2:10). Communicating from prison via a hand-delivered message, Paul assured the Ephesians that God was performing great deeds through their efforts, even while they lived under the oppressive Roman Empire. The Greek word for "handiwork" can be translated as "art." Paul says that God is like the artistic director of a human orchestra that produces glorious music.

Two thousand years later, Paul's letter inspires us to grow as servant communicators. Paul presents the gospel from the perspective of those of us who can look back and acknowledge that God saved us because we could not save ourselves. Paul explains that the Lord redeems us for "good works"—actions—that will glorify God and make a difference in the world. We are God's communicators.

Many of our communication situations seem difficult. Given my challenging background with an alcoholic father and schizophrenic mother who divorced when I was in fifth grade, I feared that I would not be a decent husband and father, let alone a grandfather. I grew up in a verbal and physical war zone. Every night I went to bed with a pillow over my head to try to silence the conflict. Fear suffocated my hope.

I have no way of explaining how I climbed out of that mess other than to say that God was with me. During my university days, God began filling my heart with gratitude for salvation and every other good thing—friends, worship, patience, and so much more. I started noticing what God was doing in and around me. I heard the rising music of Ephesians where I previously was deaf. I listened—paid attention—to God's grace, often in the places I least expected to find it. God was always there ahead of me, preparing messages in advance, signs of the kingdom of God on earth. When I played too quickly or off-key, he called me back to my seat in the orchestra and gave me more patience and skill. My woundedness from childhood became a blessing as I became particularly compassionate toward those from difficult backgrounds. Wounds that cause us to suffer now, says Henri Nouwen, "will be revealed to us later as the place where God initiated his new creation."[1]

As I have tried to capture in this book, God, through the Holy Spirit, continually sets up opportunities for us to use the gift of communication to love him and our neighbors as ourselves. As we strive to become servant communicators, we discover that God is with us, revealing opportunities, giving us courage, and filling our hearts with virtue. In Genesis, God brings the animals to Adam to see what Adam will name them (Gen. 2:19–20). Today, as always, God shows us where, when, and how to communicate for shalom in his name. God even gives us the right desire to love others. We follow Jesus into the world, seeking to be open-hearted ambassadors of God's Word. Augustine says that "what is reprehensible is not the use made of things but the user's [disordered] desires"—loving something other than God first.[2]

Do we dare desire to take our seat in God's good-works orchestra? Do we dare not? Each day we rise, wash, dress, and take up our communicative strengths and weaknesses. We enter the stage of God's creation and make our music with voices, pens, computers, cameras, and phones. When we communicate well—with excellence and compassion—our communication is magnificent; it even attracts others who seek shalom. In response, we say to ourselves and others, "This is how we are meant to live. This is like a taste of heaven on earth. Thank God for the gift of communication—of community." We pray out of gratitude as well as need.

Our communication gifts are varied, complementary, and exciting. None of us is a perfect communicator, but each of us has a crucial place in the symphony of shalom. As we study communication, we can develop our skills to serve others. We do not just learn how to exchange messages but also how to love and serve the Lord, others, and ourselves.

On my tiny university office wall hung a print of a wonderful painting by John Swanson titled "The Conductor."[3] It portrays an orchestral conductor with one arm lifted for his first cue, accompanied on stage by musicians watching him closely, waiting to begin—except for a few who are glancing at the part-specific musical scores on stands in front of them. God is ready to begin directing his disciples to play his Word. In the background of the painting are three levels of faceless orchestra-hall attendees, waiting to hear and see what "good works" the conductor and orchestra will perform. In effect, the orchestra will witness through its music.[4]

Below and to the sides of the painting on my wall, I posted photos of former and current students who have joined God's orchestra, which I called the New World Symphony. I invite you to add your photo to a wall of faith by committing yourself to be a servant communicator who defies the world's cynicism and hopelessness, taking a seat in the symphony with others and playing God-pleasing, neighbor-loving music. Each day, morning to night, the Spirit is with us, showing us the way. Paul played music in letters from prison. He probably had no idea that you and I would be reading them two thousand years later in print, let alone in apps. God is preparing our unexpected communication, one message at a time. So we give thanks by communicating faithfully. The more we do it, the more we realize that the Spirit was already there, directing our good words.

Notes

Introduction

1. Paul Tournier, *To Resist or to Surrender?*, trans. John S. Gilmour (Richmond: John Knox, 1964), 17.

2. Ryan Montague, *Divine Opportunity: Finding God in the Conversations of Everyday Life* (Grand Rapids: Credo, 2016).

3. Augustine says, "Love alone distinguishes the children of God from those of the devil." *Love One Another, My Friends: Saint Augustine's Homilies on the First Letter of John*, trans. John Leinenweber (San Francisco: Harper & Row, 1989), 48.

4. WGBHForum, "Lee Child and Stephen King Talk Jack Reacher," September 14, 2015, YouTube video, 45:45, https://www.youtube.com/watch?v=4PaxX-DTGo0. Fast-forward to about five minutes into the conversation for the reference.

5. I have tried to find an original source for this quote, but apparently something like it was so widely used in the church that no one questioned it, let alone attributed it to any one source. It was a commonplace expression.

6. Henri J. M. Nouwen, *The Way of the Heart* (New York: Ballantine, 1981), 53.

7. In my view, neither "teaching" nor "doctrine" quite gets at the thrust of this book. I would prefer either "communication" or "rhetoric," but the latter carries negative connotations today.

8. Jaroslav Pelikan, *The Vindication of Tradition* (New Haven: Yale University Press, 1984), 65.

Chapter 1: Accept the Call

1. Henri J. M. Nouwen, *The Wounded Healer: Ministry in Contemporary Society* (New York: Doubleday, 1972), 19.

2. One book that nicely covers relational aspects of being created in the image and likeness of God is Shirley C. Guthrie Jr., *Christian Doctrine*, rev. ed. (Louisville: Westminster John Knox, 1994); see esp. 198–99. James K. A. Smith says, "We bear his image by carrying out our mission to cultivate creation and invite others to find their humanity in this [gospel] Story." *You Are What You Love: The Spiritual Power of Habit* (Grand Rapids: Brazos, 2016), 98.

3. David S. Cunningham, *Faithful Persuasion: In Aid of a Rhetoric of Christian Theology* (South Bend, IN: University of Notre Dame Press, 1991), 50.

4. Marshall McLuhan, *Understanding Media: The Extensions of Man* (Cambridge, MA: MIT Press, 1994), 34.

5. James W. Carey, *Communication as Culture: Essays on Media and Society* (Boston: Unwin Hyman, 1989), 165.

6. Lesslie Newbigin, *Truth to Tell: The Gospel as Public Truth* (Grand Rapids: Eerdmans, 1991), 49.

7. T. S. Eliot, *Notes towards the Definition of Culture* (Reinbek, Germany: Rowohlt, 1961), 29.

8. Perhaps the best explanation of culture as communication can be found in Carey, *Communication as Culture*, 13–36.

9. Andy Crouch, *Culture Making: Recovering Our Creative Calling* (Downers Grove, IL: IVP Books, 2008), 12.

10. Lynn O'Shaughnessy, "New Study Shows Careers and College Majors Often Don't Match," CBS News, November 15, 2013, https://www.cbsnews.com /news/new-study-shows-careers-and-college-majors-often-dont-match; Brad Plumer, "Only 27 Percent of College Grads Have a Job Related to Their Major," *Washington Post*, May 20, 2013, https://www.washingtonpost.com/news/wonk /wp/2013/05/20/only-27-percent-of-college-grads-have-a-job-related-to-their -major.

11. Augustine, *On Christian Teaching*, trans. R. P. H. Green (New York: Oxford University Press, 1997), 23.

Chapter 2: Offer Thanks

1. Augustine, *Love One Another, My Friends: Saint Augustine's Homilies on the First Letter of John*, trans. John Leinenweber (San Francisco: Harper & Row, 1989), 73.

2. Abraham J. Heschel, *Who Is Man?* (Stanford, CA: Stanford University Press, 1965), 111, 114 (emphasis in original).

3. See Kenneth Burke, "(Nonsymbolic) Motion/(Symbolic) Action," *Critical Inquiry* 4, no. 4 (1978): 810.

4. Stephen Bullon, "In the News: One Million Words of English. (More or Less.)," *Macmillan Dictionary Blog*, 2009, http://www.macmillandictionaryblog .com/one-million-words-of-english.

5. Heschel says, "We can attain adequate understanding of man only if we think of man in human terms, *more humano*, and abstain from employing categories developed in the investigation of lower forms of life." *Who Is Man?*, 3.

6. See any edition of Em Griffin's *A First Look at Communication Theory* for a solid overview of major theories of communication. The book is now in its tenth edition (New York: McGraw-Hill, 2019).

7. Mary Oliver, "Morning Poem," in *New and Selected Poems* (Boston: Beacon, 1992), 1:107.

8. See James K. A. Smith, *Who's Afraid of Postmodernism? Taking Derrida, Lyotard, and Foucault to Church* (Grand Rapids: Baker Academic, 2006).

9. Augustine, *On Christian Teaching*, trans. R. P. H. Green (New York: Oxford University Press, 1997), 78.

10. Frederick Buechner, *Wishful Thinking: A Seeker's ABC*, rev. ed. (San Francisco: HarperSanFrancisco, 1993), 120.

11. I have been significantly influenced by speech-act theory, which seems to me to capture both how human communication works and why we are called to be responsible communicators. Communication deals not just with words and other symbols but also with what we do together with symbols.

12. Adam S. McHugh, *The Listening Life: Embracing Attentiveness in a World of Distraction* (Downers Grove, IL: IVP Books, 2015), 136.

13. Tony Campolo and Mary Albert Darling, *Connecting Like Jesus: Practices for Healing, Teaching, and Preaching* (San Francisco: Jossey-Bass, 2010), 67.

14. Kenneth Burke, *The Rhetoric of Religion: Studies in Logology* (Berkeley: University of California Press, 1970), 17–23.

Chapter 3: Be Responsible

1. For an accessible overview of the cultural mandate, I especially like John G. Stackhouse Jr., *Why You're Here: Ethics for the Real World* (New York: Oxford University Press, 2018), 14–26.

2. Abraham J. Heschel, *Who Is Man?* (Stanford, CA: Stanford University Press, 1965), 97.

3. Heschel, *Who Is Man?*, 101, 108.

4. "Specifically, man at creation is singled out as the creature who alone among earthlings is *responsible*. He alone is accountable." Nicholas Wolterstorff, *Art in Action: Toward a Christian Aesthetic* (Grand Rapids: Eerdmans, 1980), 73.

5. Eugene H. Peterson, *Subversive Spirituality*, ed. Jim Lyster, John Sharon, and Peter Santucci (Grand Rapids: Eerdmans, 1997), 23; Henri J. M. Nouwen, *Clowning in Rome: Reflections on Solitude, Celibacy, Prayer, and Contemplation* (New York: Doubleday, 1979), 103.

6. Heschel, *Who Is Man?*, 37.

7. Augustine says, "It is therefore necessary above all else to be moved by the fear of God towards learning his will: what it is that he instructs us to seek and avoid." *On Christian Teaching*, trans. R. P. H. Green (New York: Oxford University Press, 1997), 33.

Chapter 4: Address Brokenness

1. An excellent resource for addressing potential arguments is Mike Bechtle, *Dealing with the Elephant in the Room: Moving from Tough Conversations to Healthy Communication* (Grand Rapids: Revell, 2015).

2. Abraham J. Heschel, *Who Is Man?* (Stanford, CA: Stanford University Press, 1965), 112–13.

3. J. Grant Howard, *The Trauma of Transparency: A Biblical Approach to Inter-Personal Communication* (Portland, OR: Multnomah, 1979), 27.

4. Henri J. M. Nouwen, *The Way of the Heart* (New York: Ballantine, 1981), 47.

5. For more on addiction, vulnerability, and community, see Gerald G. May, *Addiction and Grace: Love and Spirituality in the Healing of Addictions* (San Francisco: HarperOne, 1988). May says that grace, including freedom from addiction, often comes to us in community (124).

6. Søren Kierkegaard, *Provocations: Spiritual Writings of Kierkegaard*, ed. Charles E. Moore (Farmington, PA: Plough, 1999), 241.

7. This is one of those quotes that appears frequently but rarely with an attribution. I use it because it appears in a well-researched book of quotations. Paul Thigpen, *A Dictionary of Quotes from the Saints* (Ann Arbor, MI: Servant, 2001), 91.

8. Robert K. Greenleaf, *On Becoming a Servant Leader*, ed. Don M. Frick and Larry C. Spears (San Francisco: Jossey-Bass, 1996), 17.

9. Blaise Pascal, *Pensées: Thoughts on Religion and Other Subjects*, trans. William Finlayson Trotter (New York: Washington Square, 1965), 37.

10. Václav Havel, *The Art of the Impossible: Politics as Morality in Practice*, trans. Paul Wilson (New York: Fromm International, 1994), 4.

11. Lewis Smedes, *Caring and Commitment: Learning to Live the Love We Promise* (New York: Harper & Row, 1989).

12. Augustine, *Confessions*, trans. Henry Chadwick (New York: Oxford University Press, 1991), 179.

13. Dietrich Bonhoeffer, *Life Together* (New York: Harper & Row, 1954), 111.

Chapter 5: Embrace Community

1. "PM Launches Government's First Loneliness Strategy," GOV.UK, last updated October 16, 2018, https://www.gov.uk/government/news/pm-launches -governments-first-loneliness-strategy.

2. James W. Carey, *Communication as Culture: Essays on Media and Society* (Boston: Unwin Hyman, 1989), 18.

3. Philosopher Nicholas Wolterstorff says that shalom is a way of living that reflects "both God's cause in the world and our human calling." *Until Justice and Peace Embrace* (Grand Rapids: Eerdmans, 1983), 72. In such a community, everyone enjoys harmonious relationships filled with delight. Shalom, or peace, is first articulated in the poetic and prophetic literature: "The wolf will live with the lamb, the leopard will lie down with the goat, the calf and the lion and the yearling together; and a little child will lead them" (Isa. 11:6). Shalom is where the "mountain of the LORD's temple" is "exalted above the hills" so that "all nations will stream to it" (Isa. 2:2).

4. See James J. O'Donnell, "A Common Quotation for 'Augustine'?," Faculty Website, Georgetown University, http://faculty.georgetown.edu/jod/augustine /quote.html.

5. John M. Gottman, *The Seven Principles for Making Marriage Work* (New York: Harmony, 1999), 17.

6. Josef Pieper, *Abuse of Language, Abuse of Power*, trans. Lothar Krauth (San Francisco: Ignatius, 1992), 21.

7. Augustine, *On Christian Teaching*, trans. R. P. H. Green (New York: Oxford University Press, 1997), 27.

8. Sissela Bok, *Lying: Moral Choice in Public and Private Life* (New York: Vintage, 1999), xxi.

Chapter 6: Be Virtuous

1. In his *Rhetoric*, Aristotle argued that the three major means of persuasion are logos, pathos, and ethos. An excellent review of Aristotle's approach to rhetoric, with application for the church, is David S. Cunningham, *Faithful Persuasion: In Aid of a Rhetoric of Christian Theology* (South Bend, IN: University of Notre Dame Press, 1991).

2. I do not include love and faithfulness here because I address them in other sections of the book.

3. Søren Kierkegaard, *Provocations: Spiritual Writings of Kierkegaard*, ed. Charles E. Moore (Farmington, PA: Plough, 1999), 319.

4. Henri J. M. Nouwen, *The Wounded Healer: Ministry in Contemporary Society* (New York: Doubleday, 1972), 66.

5. "St. Augustine of Hippo," Catholic Online, https://www.catholic.org/saints /saint.php?saint_id=418.

6. Augustine, *On Christian Teaching*, trans. R. P. H. Green (New York: Oxford University Press, 1997), 68.

7. Rabbi Joseph Telushkin, *Words That Hurt, Words That Heal: How to Use Words Wisely and Well* (New York: Perennial Current, 1998), xx.

Chapter 7: Tell Stories

1. Marilyn Chandler McEntyre, *Caring for Words in a Culture of Lies* (Grand Rapids: Eerdmans, 2009), 121.

2. Benson P. Fraser, *Hide and Seek: The Sacred Art of Indirect Communication* (Eugene, OR: Cascade Books, 2020), 4.

3. Aristotle, *Poetics*, trans. Gerald F. Else (Ann Arbor: University of Michigan Press, 1970), 5–8.

4. William D. Romanowski, *Cinematic Faith: A Christian Perspective on Movies and Meaning* (Grand Rapids: Baker Academic, 2019), 9.

5. Frederick Buechner, *Telling the Truth: The Gospel as Tragedy, Comedy, and Fairy Tale* (San Francisco: HarperSanFrancisco, 1977), 7.

6. See Robert H. Woods Jr. and Paul D. Patton, *Prophetically Incorrect: A Christian Introduction to Media Criticism* (Grand Rapids: Brazos, 2010).

7. The movie can be viewed online at https://www.jesusfilm.org/watch.html.

8. Ian I. Mitroff and Warren Bennis, *The Unreality Industry: The Deliberate Manufacturing of Falsehood and What It Is Doing to Our Lives* (New York: Oxford University Press, 1989), xvi.

9. Augustine, *On Christian Teaching*, trans. R. P. H. Green (New York: Oxford University Press, 1997), 47.

Chapter 8: Discern Media

1. Marshall McLuhan, *Understanding Media: The Extensions of Man*, 1st MIT Press ed. (Cambridge, MA: MIT Press, 1994).

2. Philip Yancey, *The Jesus I Never Knew* (Grand Rapids: Zondervan, 1995), 87.

3. The best book on oral culture is probably Walter J. Ong, *The Presence of the Word: Some Prolegomena for Cultural and Religious History* (New Haven: Yale University Press, 1967). It shaped much of my thinking about communication beginning when I was in graduate school. "Knowledge grows by hope," says Ong. "For all knowledge is only arrested dialogue, framed ultimately in speech, in communication" (315).

4. Irene Brouwer Konyndyk, *Foreign Languages for Everyone: How I Learned to Teach Second Languages to Students with Learning Disabilities* (Grand Rapids: Edenridge, 2011).

5. Fittingness is "a feature of the reality in which we all exist." Nicholas Wolterstorff, *Art in Action: Toward a Christian Aesthetic* (Grand Rapids: Eerdmans, 1980), 96.

6. Abraham J. Heschel, *Who Is Man?* (Stanford, CA: Stanford University Press, 1965), 8.

7. Augustine, *On Christian Teaching*, trans. R. P. H. Green (New York: Oxford University Press, 1997), 21.

Closing Thoughts

1. Henri J. M. Nouwen, *The Wounded Healer: Ministry in Contemporary Society* (New York: Doubleday, 1972), 96.

2. Augustine, *On Christian Teaching*, trans. R. P. H. Green (New York: Oxford University Press, 1997), 77.

3. An image is available on the artist's website at http://johnaugustswanson .com/default.cfm/PID%3D1.2-27.html.

4. The facelessness reminds me of C. S. Lewis's book *Till We Have Faces: A Myth Retold* (London: Geoffrey Bles, 1956). As I understand the book, Lewis suggests that people without faces do not yet see themselves fully. When we face Jesus directly in the mirror of the gospel, we gain faces to see that we are both deeply fallen and wonderfully redeemed persons, not just faces in an impersonal crowd.